STUDY TRIP

DIRK VIS

Psychedelics for Research and Art

Edited by Lucia Pietroiusti

Set Margins' #97

PER LA MIA LUCE

The universe is real, but you can't see it.
You have to imagine it.
Alexander Calder

Table of Contents

Part III: Integration

Extras

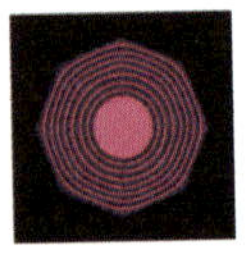

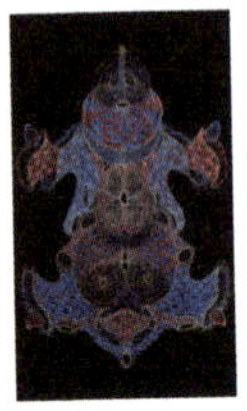

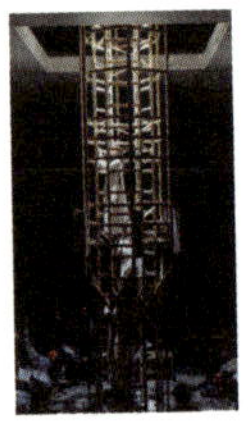

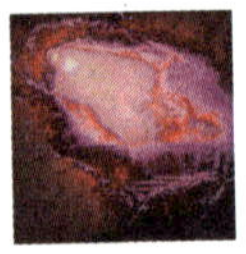

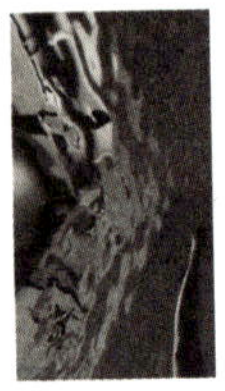

Acknowledgements

This book could not have been made without the people I tripped with: you know who you are.

Thanks to Carolyn Christov-Bakargiev, Jason Day, Jemma Foster, Philip Gorski, Aldo Kroese, Iris Lam, Sammy Lee, Senka Milutinović, Arjen Mulder, Kyrke Otto, Toine Pieters, Miriam Rasch and Shengyu Wang for their conversations, inspiration, generous suggestions and insightful critique.

Deep gratitude to Marieke van Rhijn for her therapeutic guidance. Several important questions in the diary template in the back of this book were first posed to me by her. Thanks also to Beri for her meditative experiments. To Florentino Orosco, Gerard Verschoor, and Abuelo Gregorio for their hospitality and generosity.

Thanks to the artists for granting me permission to reproduce their work.

Thanks to Robert Reinartz, Ruben Pater, Edgar Walthert and Job Wouters for their collaboration and advice on design.

Thanks to everyone at the Netherlands Institute for Advanced Study. Thanks to many of my students, who over the years joined lectures and seminars in which I developed the ideas that now make up this book. Thanks to the many others – too many to mention individually – who helped shape the ideas in this book in myriad other ways.

Thanks to Johanna Monk for her focused proofing, and generous listening.

Infinite gratitude to Lucia Pietroiusti, for all her generosity, encouragement and inspiration; for editing the text of this book; and for collaborating on the selection of artworks.

Lastly, in a book such as this, it does not feel out of place to thank the spirits of devotion, discipline, community, natureculture and many others, in all their diaphanous, dance-like, colourful brilliance, as I first recognised them – as a young student – in the tiny, face-like, more-than-human features hidden in plain sight in the leaves, rocks, streams and clouds painted on the pages of Ferdowsi's illuminated *Book of Kings*.

Introduction

We can undertake a psychedelic trip in order to study the world. This idea is simple enough, and depending on its context, it is also ancient and revolutionary in equal measure. A psychedelic research practice can lead to all forms of art as ways of sharing our findings. 'To study', in this case, does not refer to any formal academic or scientific pursuit. Instead, a student here is understood as someone devoted and eager to learn.

A study trip is not therapeutic; it is not for self-growth; it is not for entertainment; it is not monitored scientifically as part of psychiatric or pharmacological research; it is not to relax; it is not for subversion; it is not countercultural; it is not escapist; it is not for collecting artistic material;

it is not for productivity, and neither is it undertaken in order to gain or work with otherworldly powers. A study trip needs a way of understanding psychedelics that does not necessarily exclude these aspects, but places them within another perspective. For a study trip, all preconceived intentions and goals are let go of, in order to find new intent, new questions, for the curiosity of the student and the benefit of their communities.

Many have studied psychedelics with psychedelics. If through psychedelics you study psychedelics, what you will eventually learn about is you, studying. If you use psychedelics primarily for entertainment, you will come to feel hollow: you will have become the entertainment. Taking psychedelics to heal yourself will end up showing you a version of you that appears whole, yet at risk of buying into the consumerist notion of an individual solution.

Of course, scientific research into psychedelics is important for many reasons, but it usually cannot take full account of the outcomes of studying through psychedelics. Psychedelic experiences are weird, unverifiable, different for everyone and with every session, and almost impossible to describe. There is confusion, taboo and mystery around them. This book intends to clarify confusion and celebrate mystery.

For as long as humans have existed, they have ingested psychedelic substances and engaged in ecstatic techniques, although we may never definitively know why they did so. The historical ways in which psychedelics have been used by Indigenous communities the world over are so diverse, and many worldviews and contexts so distant from our own, that many ways of doing psychedelics remain virtually inaccessible. At home, you may enjoy rituals imported from far away, or you may travel to encounter local ones, which promise authentic and meaningful experiences, but these will inevitably also be very different from those same rituals performed in their situated and traditional cultural contexts. Different landscapes – just like different worldviews – exclude the possibility that experiences may be replicated exactly.

I tried psychedelics of all kinds, for many reasons and for decades, but I did so mostly ignorantly. I travelled to far-flung corners of the Earth and stumbled upon psychedelic ways that sometimes made much more sense to me than what I'd known up to that point, while at other times they remained deeply impenetrable. But to study is to simply keep on taking steps into the unknown; letting go of obstructing assumptions you may hold; taking care not to lose too much, but teetering on the shaky edges of what you know. I have more experience with certain techniques and substances than others, and this might give the book a particular character, yet the text focuses on those aspects and experiences that the wider range of psychedelic practices can and often do share.

The knowledge, skills and rituals related to Western-European Indigenous psychedelic plants and rituals have been repressed for centuries, and are only slowly being rediscovered over multiple generations. In the Western-European province I come from, farmers have become managerial-knowledge workers who control machines. The use of local, medicinal fungi and herbs that can be healthy – if expertly prepared – has been made almost impossible, often even criminalised. Simultaneously, large, illegal chemical labs – in the same countryside – produce industrial quantities of powerful, synthetic psychoactive drugs, for an international clientele. All of this gives you and me not only the possibility, but perhaps also the responsibility, to reinvent psychedelic practices for our own cultural context, moving away from appropriation or extraction, and relying more on reconnecting to the changing land. The knowledge and skills involved are certainly ancient, because they connect to practices that are thousands of years old, but they are also brand new, because they keep on needing to be reinvented as their contexts change.

Besides art, many great works of philosophy, chemistry and engineering have likely been inspired by the use of psychedelics, even if their role has almost always gone unacknowledged. There is no academic field that explicitly conducts studies through the medium or method of psychedelics. A study undertaken through psychedelic practices – it may be suggested – could be called a science of not-knowing. In other words, it is a form of research that is related to traditional epistemology, the study of knowledge, yet is fundamentally different from it: an epistemology of the weird. In this way, its most concentrated expression may be found in the form of art, which is, by necessity, a way of knowing the world otherwise.

Studying through psychedelics means considering the world composed not of objects outside of yourself, but of subjectivities that you can temporarily share in. If you look at a candle long enough – its visual rhythms mirroring in your brain – you can feel yourself turning into a flame. The vanishing forms remind you that you can also see with your eyes closed. The body slowly changes from instrument to music. These days an endless flickering point of light is more likely to be wit- nessed on a screen, its maker burning through data and algorithms, creating enchanting circles, lines and patterns. Stare at it long enough, and it might come to stand in for the powerfully colourful thing that emerges between you and all the other beings you are truly connected with.

This book's intended audience is first and foremost the relatively small group of people in any community that wants to study through tripping or facilitate such activity; all those artists, creatives, students, adventurers, psychonauts, psychologists and mystics who use psychedelics because they want to, and who want to grow in their work. Secondly, this book is intended for everyone who would like to be able to integrate occasional experiences better in their life and work, using their creative talents consciously, no matter their profession. Thirdly, because of the inherently psychedelic nature of art, you don't need to take or do psychedelics at all to be able to enjoy the many different perspectives on art and creativity that this book surfaces. Even without actively engaging with psychedelics, learning a robust vocabulary on alternative ways of knowing is – I believe – essential for anyone working creatively.

There are small pockets of psychedelic practitioners in the margins everywhere. There are commercial sellers of particular legal psychedelics, there are pharmacological or psychiatric researchers in the sciences, and there are religious cults and sects that legally use psychedelics. If and how they might become part of a wider, more momentous cultural shift towards a use of psychedelics for the explicit purpose of study remains unknown. As a result – and this I find to be one of the most exciting aspects of writing this today – this book describes a scene, and attempts to address a community, that might just be emerging.

As you go through the book, you'll find descriptions of different communities relevant for psychedelic study: the group of people you trip with, the group you share your dreams with, the group you share your creative work with, but also the communities of more-than-human beings, plant, animal and fungal life, that are involved in the production of psychedelic substances, as well as those you may encounter on your study trips. If there is a common thread throughout this book, it is this: learning through psychedelic study is about how to reconnect with the living land. That may include learning to reconnect to those who think differently.

I belong to a unique historical period and a set of specific communities that largely ignores how the sacred can be accessed and shared in society. In many ways, this worldview is a very strange outlier. Having some training as an engineer, but working mostly with language, my wish was to become something for which there was no explicit school: a technician of the sacred. For too long, we have pretended that the sacred didn't exist, or that it would be better if it didn't. I aim to use any permissiveness that may still be found within my own cultural context to guide you through every aspect of psychedelics, performed as study. The aim is to be a tripsitter of sorts, even at a distance.

Dirk Vis
Rotterdam/London, 2026

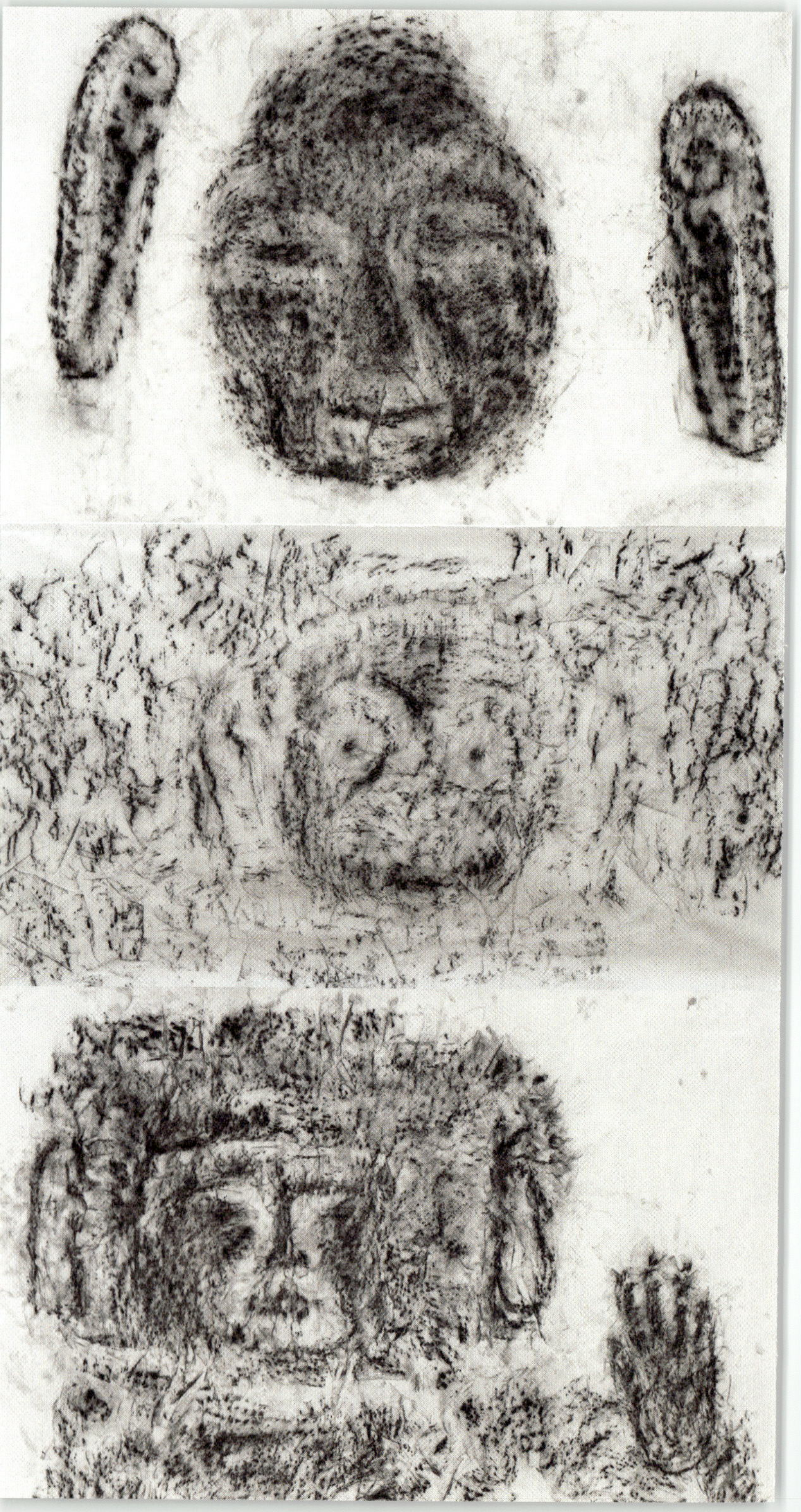

How to Read this Book

This book is structured in three parts: *Preparation*, *Celebration* and *Integration*, each covering the most important topics that come up before, during or after a study trip, respectively. You can read it from cover to cover, or jump directly to your chapter of choice.

Perhaps you are preparing for a study trip and want to dive into part one. Or you find yourself reflecting on a past experience, and would like to re-read a particular chapter from part three. In part two, you might find elements worth remembering while in psychedelic celebration.

Preparation and *Integration* are just as important as *Celebration*. If doing psychedelics is opening a portal, you'll also need to know how to close it again, because a permanently open portal is indistinguishable from madness.

Every chapter of this book covers a single subject, and it begins with an artwork. Together, these artworks form a visual essay, and each individual artwork reinforces the chapter's core subject on the relation between psychedelics and creativity. No attempt has been made to be exhaustive. The texts contain experiential knowledge expressed through discursive argument, but also through rhythm, melody, movement and metaphor. It is also a work of the imagination, as befits a work of ecstatic knowledge, the kind that cannot be empirically verified. It must be intuited, wished for, imagined, danced or felt, in order to be understood. The knowledge in this book is itself often weird, at times incomplete, open to change, non-systematic, and messy. This kind of knowledge does not set off with the idea that, eventually, everything is knowable, if only you work and study harder. Instead, it rests on the intuition that for everything you can learn, you also become aware of something else that is and remains unknown.

While this book is as much about psychedelic techniques as it is about substances, for some aspects it is most relevant to focus on substances. This book does not describe the effects of specific psychedelics, however, or how to find or prepare them, even though the trippier parts of every chapter are each dedicated to a different technique or substance. You will not find detailed instructions on using substances or performing techniques, such as breathwork or meditation, because this kind of information is al- ready widely available, and it is different depending on where you are.

Each chapter has a single endnote that provides more context. Reading these notes is not strictly necessary for a study trip. Nevertheless, they forge connections to the work of those artists and writers that have inspired ideas in this book.

For more detailed and in-depth context, this book is accompanied by a reader – *The Library of Not-Knowing* – an anthology that contains many of the references used here, and more, newly contextualised. This *Library* bridges work from scholars and artists, and spans genres and origins, from pre-modern, Indigenous, countercultural, urban and neo-shamanic, to art-historical and epistemological. It can be considered a reading list for a shadow curriculum on psychedelic study.

Study Trip is a choir of several voices. The authoritative voice is that of the teacher we all have within ourselves. Another voice is more contemplative, and prefers to ask questions. This book can be read as a dialogue between these two: between the speaker and the listener, the maker and the observer, the teacher and the student. Between your regular, everyday conscious you, and a deeper you that listens.

Lastly, a note of caution. As the core of all psychedelics, meditation can in most cases be practiced without any danger. But depending on your health, situation, and location, the use of psychedelic substances may not be suitable for you. In different countries, different substances can also be illegal. This book does not condone psychedelic experimentation that is illegal, or that is done without proper guidance. Most importantly, psychedelic practices cannot be learned from a book alone, and always need to be performed under the guidance of professionals.

Note to *Acknowledgements, Introduction* & *How to Read this Book*

In *My Spiritual Evolution*, a non-fiction story that describes the results of his encounters with DMT and his research into near-death experiences, author Tao Lin recounts a vision in which a being made of light reminds him of the importance of only two things in life: 'loving others and acquiring knowledge'. While Lin never explicitly refers to psychedelics as a form of study, I find his formulation to be a perfect description of what the aims of a study trip could be.

This idea connects to scientist Carlo Rovelli's position on 'studying', whereby you are always finding a balance between letting go of what you know in order to find new things, and holding on to what is known in order to ground your work. Therefore, any study through psychedelics is by necessity indebted to all those past and ongoing studies undertaken on the subject of psychedelics. It is only through such academic research that a well-informed study trip – a study through psychedelics – is possible.

If the aim of a study trip is 'acquiring knowledge', we are not talking here about ordinary knowledge. Historian of the sacred Philip Gorski suggests we think about these forms of knowing as an 'epistemology of the weird', and I would suggest that it is also a bit like 'learned ignorance', or, as we will see in the last three chapters of this book, cultivating 'not-knowing'.

While a fixed definition of psychedelics, or study, might not be helpful, my description of everything a study trip is not, is much indebted to poet and philosopher Kyrke Otto's comment, that a study trip is a particular way of looking at psychedelics among many. As it is, there have been countless perspectives on psychedelics, including across Indigenous communities worldwide.

As regards 'learning how to love', this, to me, is something that, in a study trip, has a chance to happen at planetary scale: through psychedelics, we learn a love that has as much to do with environmental consciousness and planetary health as it does with a state of emotional intensity.

A fundamental inspiration for this book is the work of Jim Corbett. In his *Sanctuary for all Life*, Corbett describes something I had been doing long before I could describe or name it: an utterly practical version of mysticism, one that accepts that some things can be known and some things not, and one that connects inward training with outward connections, in a down-to-Earth quest to rejoin the living land.

'Inward training' itself is a term I borrow from the work of scholar Harold D. Roth on the Taoist text *Nei-Yeh*, an ancient Chinese poem describing meditative techniques.

That such inward training can also be done through artistic work is exemplified by *Quantum*, a work by Jennifer and Kevin McCoy. This is a code-based work, an animated GIF, a relatively simple file, presenting an ongoing, abstract cycle of birth, death, and rebirth. *Quantum* has been described, too, as a picture of the moment of creation of the work itself. People have seen in the *Quantum* image a heartbeat, a mandala, a flame.

The work *Rock 'n Feel* of ikkibawiKrrr is based on ancient Buddhist stone statues. Using paper and charcoal, they trace hands, ears, garments and faces from these immense sculptures. The drawings afford us a 'tactile view' of the stones, almost a sense of presence. While we may never know what moved the original sculptors to make their works, we reconnect to them, by asking questions about their practices.

Image on p.10: Ferdowsi, The Feast of Sada, *ca. 1525. Opaque watercolour, ink, silver and gold on paper. From* The Book of Kings. *Made available under the Creative Commons CC0 1.0 Universal Public Domain Dedication.*

Image on p.12: Jennifer and Kevin McCoy, Quantum, *2014. Animated GIF, minted on the Namecoin blockchain. Courtesy of the artists.*

Images on p.22: ikkibawiKrrr, Rock 'n Feel, *2024. Charcoal on paper, 15 pieces. Photo by ikki, courtesy of the artists.*

Part I: Preparation

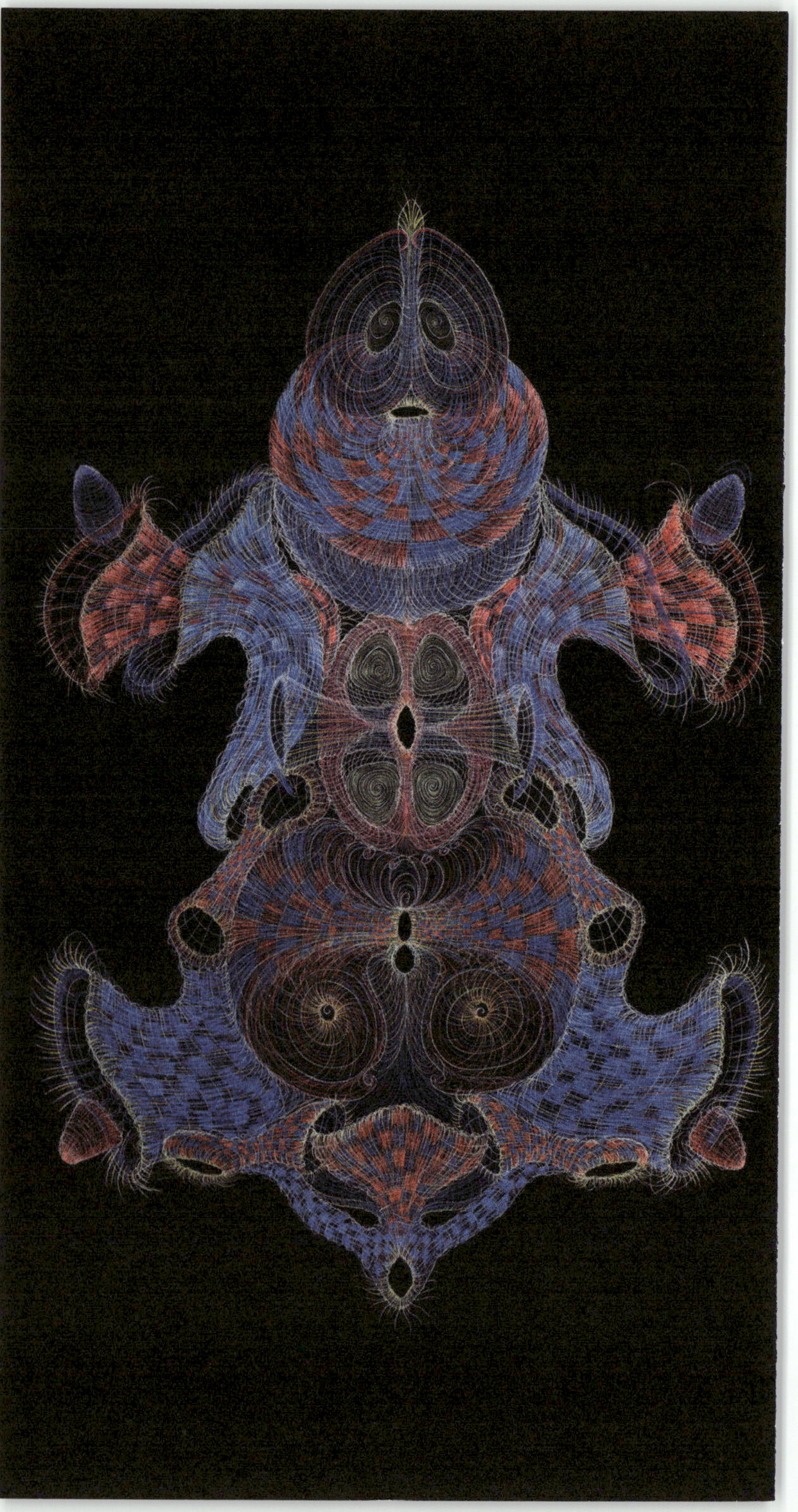

What Is Intention?

A study trip celebrates a question. The conscious intention at the start of a study trip is the abandonment of all intention: you can only find a question when you are not already preoccupied by one that was formulated by your ego or by institutions. Letting go of intent is exactly how you will find new intent.

If you don't know your intentions, psychedelics will show them to you. If you do, psychedelics will take you to a place where you don't know them anymore, where your intentions meet with those of the living worlds around you.

The word 'psychedelic' literally means: that which makes the mind or soul manifest. It turns the world upside down and inside out, because you're suddenly seeing around you what otherwise remains hidden;

a world of phenomena that are not yet explicit, not yet manifested, only manifesting. This includes your own feelings and thoughts as part of the collective of all feelings and thoughts. In other words, a world of pure intention.

Intention can be shared, but not measured; it can be hidden, but not falsified. Your will can align with an intention, but you cannot will an intention into being. Your will is powerless in psychedelic space-time, but you can attune your attention to an intention already out there. You move through intention with and by attention only.

For instance, your ego cannot decide to stay longer in substance-induced psychedelic space, or to get out faster. But should you come upon the intention to leave with full attention – perhaps because of some emergency – you will be out of your trip instantly. Similarly, self-centred will cannot impose a longer meditation, but should you align with the intention to stay longer, you might be able to stay indefinitely.

The highest form of attention is completely dedicated, surrendered to whatever may come, in faith, witnessing all things with love. No status, money, power or fame can come from it. What you encounter is revelation, a breakthrough. It remains a mystery whether the seeing itself might already have an effect. Even if you cannot go in with any expectations or plans, you might find there entire scenes or constructions, that you can help come into being when you return.

What intentions might a bear, a lemur or a millipede have when they trip? Would a tree ever wonder what it might be like to walk? The visions are non-linguistic, but full of meaning. The entire world is animated with life, communicating synaesthetically.

It seems even a chair wants to speak. Ideas, feelings, emotions or sensations that you might have long cherished, or that you might not have known before at all, can now come over you, move through you, in iridescent, tingling, ghostly forms, lighting up with flashing, delightful insights, heating your body up as they energise you, and tell you wordlessly how to stay attuned.

Are you ready, too, to open up to any suffering you might observe? Can you bear witness to it? Can you learn to stay present without engaging, until you align with exactly those intentions that are beneficial for you and yours? And so, in giving up conscious intention before a study trip, you may find you align with other, unconscious, deeper intuitions. You may study childhood memories, a bodily pain – of yours or someone else's – or particular, alien presences.

This is how creative work can grow, as well. There is an unspoken question at the heart of every artwork: something you work towards, hold space for, by lingering in a state of openness. Something you might know, but might not yet be able to formulate. This is similar to attuning your attention towards a specific intention on a study trip. Psychedelics facilitate what may happen in creativity, too: a form of attention so full that your ego disappears. Whether you do it once in a lifetime, every week, or multiple times daily, the purpose of a psychedelic session is to regenerate the world, which is another way of saying: experiencing the intention to co-create, which you share with everything around you.

Note to *What Is Intention?*

Describing the cosmologies of specific Indigenous groups he worked with, philosopher David Abram writes (in *The Spell of the Sensuous*): 'The manifested [...] is that aspect of phenomena already evident to our senses, while the manifesting is that which is not yet explicit, not yet present to the senses, but which is assumed to be psychologically gathering itself toward manifestation within the depths of all sensible phenomena.' What you feel, think and desire are a part of this collective desiring and preparing. Human intention, he goes on, especially in communal ceremony, contributes directly to becoming manifested.

Simone Weil is absolutely clear on intention, attention and will, and in *Gravity and Grace*, she writes: 'We have to try to cure our faults by attention and not by will... Attention, taken to its highest degree, is the same thing as prayer. It presupposes faith and love... Attention alone – that attention which is so full that the "I" disappears – is required of me. I have to deprive all that I call "I" of the light of my attention and turn it on to that which cannot be conceived.'

It will not be a surprise to you, that such attention is prevalent in the creative process also. The artistic process of Sammy Lee can come close to that of a kind of detective: she produces forms through cymatics, or audio resonance in water, in combination with LED lights and 3D-printed shapes that function as containers for the water. The resulting visuals are eerie, ghostly and completely analog. As the resulting shapes change according to her play with variables (sound, shape, light), results can look uncannily like entities one might encounter during a study trip. These images, in turn, become blueprints for life-sized, hand-drawn sentinel figures.

Meeting a specific presence like that, or revisiting it later, can be the kind of intention you learn to attune to. In this chapter I have also drawn on other examples of intentionality, some based on a conversation with philosopher and writer Jason Day.

Image on p.28: Sammy Lee, Birthing the world on the turtle's back (what's the rush?), *2025. Pastel on paper, 250 x 150 cm. Photo: Andrew Judd, courtesy of the artist.*

A Dance of Substance and Technique

The words psychedelic, psychoactive, psychotropic, holotropic, entheogenic, and hallucinogenic can be used to mean the same thing, but in different contexts. This variety reflects how much complexity and confusion there is about them. However, some things are clear: some psychedelic substances can have similar effects as psychedelic techniques; the same methods can have different effects on different people; and the same methods can have very different effects on the same person at different moments.

Techniques of ecstasy aren't limited to substances: prolonged multi-media exposure, clubbing, breathing exercises, and working with relics made from natural objects, are only a few contemporary ways of reaching altered states of consciousness. You can find more or less subtle trance states in countless activities: running, fasting, yoga, sweat lodges, sensory deprivation tanks, sex, dancing, singing, art, prayer, deep listening, being in nature, spending a full-moon night in the forest, staying in the dark. A psychedelic session can involve any combination of these. Mixing techniques with substances can be done in infinite ways: a relic might send you into a deep trance, while a substance pulls you out of it, and vice versa. There is no fixed method, no predictable outcome. There may be as many ways of reaching psychedelic spacetime as there are people doing it. And no two aesthetic trance states are the same. You might reach it instantly and abruptly, or very subtly over many attempts spread out over prolonged periods. Colours appear to hold depth. Sounds come alive. Time dilates and contracts.

The root of all psychedelic practice is meditation. There are many methods to go about it, yet meditation preferably happens without any method at all. Psychedelic trips can be interpreted as substance-induced meditations, aided by the ancient technology of plant medicine. They may lead to mental states that you can revisit without substances. Similarly, meditative techniques of ecstasy can help you train capacities and awareness for safe substance-based journeys.

If psychedelic substances are gateway drugs, they are gateways to reconnecting to nature and meditation. Any narcotic or repressive drug becomes unattractive. More synthetically induced ecstasy – even though it may introduce profound states of mind to be revisited later – runs the risk of bypassing or depleting – instead of training – your inner, ecstatic capacity, and can be quickly set aside for less processed substances. Similarly, highly scripted and forced techniques may be slowly let go in favour of softer yet more powerful ones.

You may not need any psychedelic substance or technique to achieve altered states at all. This realisation is almost a prerequisite for successfully doing psychedelics, protecting you against the risk of becoming psychologically dependent. Through your own mind, imagination and artistic creation, you can reach the same or similar states. Psychedelics are not even a shortcut to such experiences, because doing them successfully, safely, and in connection and reciprocity, necessitates just as much work, integration and training.

Doing psychedelic sessions regularly becomes a study trajectory, a high pilgrimage, where each time, you continue where you last left off. Even if you try a substance only once, it will integrate itself within your wider journey, in subtle ways. A healthy psychedelic practice might involve both substances and techniques, as well as creative work. You can reflect on how these activities change for you over time. The transformation of experiences, thoughts and emotions through artistic work facilitates an important balancing factor, allowing the integration of any unprocessed questions that substance-induced psychedelic study trips might bring up.

However you do it, a study trip is also a way of acknowledging that however good you might have become at it, you are entering a reality that will necessarily remain unknown; where any attempt at full understanding or coherent explaining will always prove futile.

Note to *A Dance of Substance and Technique*

There are infinite ways to describe and reach altered states. 'Going down into the cathedral,' for instance, is how divers refer to plunging under the ice in order to study marine life, in Werner Herzog's documentary *Encounters at the End of the World*.

Psychedelic explorer and dolphin researcher John C. Lilly would famously combine the wildest techniques and substances, such as using LSD in a sensory deprivation tank, alongside the dolphins in his lab.

Among many artists and mystics, poet H.D. (in *Visions and Ecstasies*) wrote about the visionary states she experienced spontaneously, without taking or practicing any psychedelic substance or technique. Having lived through severe pain in a world torn apart by war and death, alongside a troubled private life, she wrote beautifully and with deep honesty about the altered states of consciousness she reached, mostly in isolation. For her, these states were productive, and helped her creative process.

That such visionary states are accessible without any techniques or substances is the main premise of the science-fiction novel *Starmaker* by Olaf Stapledon. After accidentally discovering a particular ability, the narrator of the book ventures with his mind throughout the known and unknown universe on a 'high pilgrimage'.

Fiction or not, being open to such states without any method, technique or substance is how Jiddu Krishnamurti describes meditation.

That substance and technique are always connected is visible in the work of writer and artist Henri Michaux. Michaux produced many drawings on mescaline, a cactus-based psychedelic drug. The artist was studying mescaline itself, a self-referential study trip. He speculated it could be used to study diverse states of mind, such as madness. Studying madness from the inside – as in,

beginning from the experience of madness – is one example of the kind of unverifiable, non-empirical way that one can study through psychedelics. In the introduction to Michaux' *Selected Writings*, Octavio Paz writes that by studying mescaline, Michaux allowed mescaline to study him. Years after his experiments, Michaux would be able to make similar drawings from a sober state, reaching an altered state of consciousness simply through drawing. Watching his different drawings over the years, one can observe him getting better at it: holding the process of drawing together while being in a psychedelic state, then learning to decompose and recompose himself in relation to the unity and wholeness, as well as madness, he experienced around him.

Jeremy Shaw's *Phase Shifting Index* is an installation comprising a seven-channel video projection, sound and lights. We see archival videos of people moving, dancing and gesticulating in different kinds of trance, while a voiceover gives the videos the appearance of ethnographic documentaries. At the climax of the work, all seven videos fall in line in a single choreography of ecstatic movement, followed by a synchronised abstraction into animation, light and colour.

This work is also, indirectly, a comment on the conjuring role of art itself. When all seven separate videos suddenly align, the unifying sound, video and colours catch you off-guard, allowing for a kind of internal 'phase shift', an echo of what you are watching people experience on screen. It puts the videos' archival nature into question, as you discover you have been watching a piece of fiction. The impossibly utopian desires on screen are suddenly no longer relegated to the space of madness or religious fervour, but belong to the realm of the imagination.

Image on p.34: Jeremy Shaw, Phase Shifting Index, *2020 (still). Seven-channel HD-video, 35'19". Courtesy of the artist.*

Why Psychedelic Study?

Study isn't often thought of as surrender, dedication or love. Effort and eagerness towards knowledge, yes, but knowledge is usually treated as something that can be packaged, used, and commodified. Yet, there are other ways of understanding knowledge: to know something can mean to be able to attribute intentionality to it. Knowing your place in relation to what is studied is also knowledge. There are as many different forms of knowing, as there are forms of study.

The empirical, scientific and technological sciences mostly study objects. But the subjective experience of the things that are being studied is equally necessary in order for the study itself to have any meaning. All study has a subjective element: it's your vision, your drive, that will propel your to undertake the experiment in the first place. This visionary aspect of study is part of its subtly psychedelic side. Another way of saying this, is that there is an art to all study.

Science looks for answers to solve problems that initially appear mysterious. Art celebrates mystery by problematising answers and expressing questions. One person can perform both of these roles, because ultimately, art and science are two sides of the same thing. Subjective study is expressed through art, where the psychedelic aspect of observation is not so subtle anymore, and becomes one of its key characteristics.

Art is not a form of thinking per se: it is a form of being, yet it can also be considered a way of knowing. This is not the kind of knowledge that can be proven right or wrong, however. It is a kind of knowledge of the side of things that cannot be known. We can call this not-knowing.

Psychedelics, whether very subtly approached through dreaming, meditation or reflection, or whether actively induced through practicing techniques or taking substances, are portals to study. Psychedelic study is not mysticism, even if many experiences are difficult or appear impossible to describe. It is highly practical, and you can be very clear about what you do not know. It is the study of subjects, of experiences close to and far from your own, and it finds results in the shape of questions. Of course, just as empirical fieldwork can lead to visions, a psychedelic trip may bring clarity to an objective experiment or construction. But at the heart of psychedelic study are the immense mysteries that surround us. All you can do with those is learn to articulate the ways in which to ask about them. If the goal of objective study is to learn to understand, the goal of subjective study may be to learn to love.

A hand slowly carves through wood, searching for the slightest change in resistance. With every breath, every tap, it moves deeper, one layer further. In our human experience of time, earlier versions of ourselves disappear from view. But linger enough near a tree trunk and time is re-imagined: the years follow each other, yet remain present simultaneously within you. Time doesn't always have to be linear, nor is it gone completely once it passes. A new sapling is exposed. Newly free, it can suddenly breathe, liberated from seemingly impenetrable layers. What might life have been like in an untamed forest? Was there ever a home, in an unfarmed land, where trees, waters and rocks were as alive as you and me?

Inner study: you are already doing it, you've always done it, every night, as you dream deeply. You've been doing it during daydreaming, too, during rest, therapy, hikes, holidays, festivals. Any time you were able to make space for any of those unanswerable questions. It's one of the oldest stories: you go into a cave, a desert or a forest – literal or metaphorical – long enough to realise all is illusion, and when you return, you bring this awareness back with you.

Note to *Why Psychedelic Study?*

How objective and subjective forms of study relate to one another is eloquently described in novelist John Fowles' autobiographical essay *The Tree*, which has informed many of my thoughts. Equally beautiful and clear are the writings on the matter by physicist and author Carlo Rovelli. Specifically, Rovelli agrees with Kant's affirmation that the subject of knowledge and its object are inseparable.

I am also deeply inspired by, and grateful for, the words of Yanomami shaman Davi Kopenawa, as transcribed by Bruce Albert in their book *The Falling Sky*: 'I did not learn to think about the things of the forest by setting my eyes on paper skins. I saw them for real by drinking my elders' breath of life with the yakoana powder they gave me': here, studying the environment happens through ritual, psychedelics and a deep connection with the ancestors.

Many anthropologists and artists have also engaged with shamanic practices. Artist Ursula Biemann describes in *The Forest Mind* how the Amazonian shaman who enters the 'medicine state' enters a relationship with the unseen world. She calls this a way of learning 'from the inside'. To know something well, according to such a study, is to be able to attribute intentionality to it, thus understanding it as a subject. In this context, knowledge is a property inherent to the environment. Here, 'knowing' means becoming part of a field of meaningful relations, i.e. sensing or understanding your place in the wider ecology.

Artist Giuseppe Penone approaches such relations through his work, too. Many of his works take hundreds of hours to make, and time can take on a role of material and medium in the process. Penone invites us to, as he puts it, 'rediscover a forest'. It is true, as philosopher Emanuele Coccia also suggests, that trees and time have a very intricate, complex relationship to one another: 'Wood is the anatomical equivalent of a multiple "I" that manages to rise constantly next to its own death.' Many of his descriptions echo psychedelic insight around ego-dissolution.

Penone employs what I like to call subtle psychedelic techniques in his sculptures and writings to reach an altered state of mind, in which this interconnection becomes manifest: 'I feel the forest breathing. I hear the slow, inexorable growth of the wood, I match my breathing to that of the green world around me, I feel the flow of the tree around my hand placed against the trunk. The altered sense of time makes what is solid, liquid, and what is liquid, solid.'

Image on p.40: Giuseppe Penone, Albero porta - cedro, *2012. Cedar, 316 x 105 x 105 cm. Photo: Josh White/JWPictures.com, courtesy of the artist.*

Study Is Ceremony

After hours of rhythmic movement, focused on breath, in a dance of yogic, martial arts-like gestures, in a dark space with colourful lights – you exercise your body until you forget it exists, until everything feels new, yet you remember this place: whether it was a club, a cave, or around a campfire; whether it was last week, last year, or in a memory from a life you're sure was not yours. This ritual moment is connected to all other similar moments, outside of time.

This intuition of repetition is one factor that allows celebration to become ceremony. Regularity – more than frequency – also relieves you of any pressure to perform now, because you know you can always return to it.

There aren't any universal, prescribed psychedelic rituals, liturgies, prayers, holy days, or sacraments.

Available to all, any psychedelic study trip – whether induced through movement, breath or substances, and whether it is collectively celebrated, or individually performed – insists on openness, rejects secrecy, and has no esoteric initiations or confirmations. There is no institutionalised psychedelic priesthood; there is no holy scripture; there are no prophets.

DJs might perform a function in contemporary, urban cultures, that comes very close to that of the shaman, yet also actors, musicians, priests, psychologists, poets and writers in their own different ways can make use of techniques of ecstasy. They all have in common that they develop techniques for stepping out of ordinary, worldly life, into an otherworldly, psychedelic moment. In celebration, all work to plan, build, and get ahead in the world stops. You step out of the structures that define everyday life, in order to observe and celebrate them, in a resting state.

Sometimes rest can be wildly explosive. But a study trip is not a party. A key difference between the altered state of psychedelics, and a merely festive, intoxicated state, is relationality: are the toils of worldly life being repressed and drowned out, or are they being recognised, celebrated and let go of in loving connection, through ceremony?

Psychedelics will never fail to show you what your life is devoted to, which is why they can often be confronting. Going into any deep study trip will make you pass through a dread equivalent to what would be caused by the loss of everything you love, own, have become and have come to know. A ceremony, however modest, can create the time and space necessary to face up to this.

Ceremony is always also concrete, it consists of social, musical, verbal or visual acts. Such aesthetic gestures, as forms of serious play, mark the place and time of celebration. They open and close, allowing the movement from preparation to celebration, and from celebration to integration. They mark the magic circle.

Any ecstatic session can become a study trip when you bring into it aspects of a sacrament: particular actions, words, objects or foodstuffs to summon a spiritual reality. Ceremonial aesthetics can help manifest a certain type, or direction, of the psychedelic experience, and they can shorten or prolong it. In psychedelic study, the ceremony is one of the few elements that can actively, consciously be designed. There is no fixed, dogmatic way in which this needs to be done, and there can be no authority in these matters, except through every participant's self-surrendered intention. Rather than coming up with ever-more complex rituals, the point is to create celebrations that help recognise and face the state of all current relations.

In a gallery or a church, erected where a forest once stood, the interior architecture of the space becomes a large resonance chamber. Human and more-than-human sounds blend, and the collective sings as if it were a single body. Your being reveals its ethereal aspects, through identification with breath and sound; the people around you show up as clouds of light; ideas, thoughts and intuitions also appear alive; colourful auras, works of the mind for the mind, making awareness visible. Suddenly, every single gesture is again full of meaning.

Note to *Study Is Ceremony*

The title of this chapter is inspired by *Research Is Ceremony*, a book by Shawn Wilson on Indigenous research methods. His thesis is that the shared aspect of an Indigenous ontology and epistemology is relationality. Wilson suggests guidelines for a research practice that is relevant for all, particularly within psychedelic study: 'All research needs to be based in a community context (be relational) and has to demonstrate respect, reciprocity and responsibility to all relationships involved in the research (and be accountable as it is put into action).'

A psychedelic practice that is intent on study can be called a 'research practice' in an artistic context. Ceremony plays a crucial role in psychedelic methods, as I suggest in this chapter.

What happens during exercises in letting go is closely related to experiences described by mystic Simone Weil. In *Decreation*, she writes: 'Renunciation demands that we should pass through anguish equivalent to that which would be caused in reality by the loss of all loved beings and all possession, including our faculties and attainments in the order of intelligence and character, our opinions, beliefs concerning what is good, what is stable, etc.'

I've learned a lot from Jim Corbett, who proposes that sabbatical moments are to a community what meditation is to an individual. In *Sanctuary for all Life*, he writes that what he calls 'Divine Presence' in the human-made world, can only reside among us briefly, sabbatically.

One's inner, spiritual life, he writes, is not disconnected from the community's outer ways of living. Corbett dedicated his life and writings to grassroots, collective organising of a religious life in the wilderness, and while he did not advocate for the use of psychedelics, a study trip is a journey into wildlands, too.

Holly Herndon's *Starmirror* is a training session and a performance in one: a choir, alongside amateur singers, come together and sing newly composed hymns, generated by Herndon and Matt Dryhurst's AI-model trained on *Ordo Virtutum*, a work by 12th-century composer and mystic Hildegard von Bingen. The singers perform in turn and in tandem with artificially generated hymns. The performance as a whole can be seen as a ceremony. It allows everyone present to perform a kind of inner study, through the physical processes of singing, breath regulation and togetherness, while participating in a reflection on the role of technology in their lives.

These examples use different ways to open and close, use and demarcate the magic circle, a concept that is most clearly expressed in Johan Huizinga's classic text *Homo Ludens*.

Image on p.46: Holly Herndon, 'Starmirror Training Performance', Starmirror, *2025. Ensemble supported by Kammerchor der Humboldt-Universität zu Berlin. Part of the exhibition Holly Herndon & Mat Dryhurst –* Starmirror *at KW Institute for Contemporary Art, Berlin, 2025. Photo: Frank Sperling, courtesy of the artist.*

Who Is Asking the Questions Here?

If study trips are the dreaming part at the heart of all forms of learning, this part is not often acknowledged, except perhaps in creative work: here the focus can be on imaginal findings, on questions, open to interpretation. It's not even you who is asking these questions: you merely find them, that is, they come to you, they come up in you.

Depending on your context and tradition, questions may be posed by a landscape; through the experience of an ocean of shared consciousness; by a living image; or by a psychedelic substance addressed as an ally. Even the most empiricist, reductionist approach to substances bestows active chemical compounds with a certain agency, one you can experience as liveliness around you. What would a fungus like to know? What traces does a tree leave within you? If a river is alive, how do you meet it?

Psychedelic study is a cultivation, like exploration in an artist's studio, of the ecstatic. Whether subtle or strong, induced or spontaneous, ecstasy is the ability to offer up the self unconditionally, while remaining present to witness what happens. Psychedelics eat the self, in the sense that the self becomes like food to the visions. There is a form of knowing in eating and being eaten, of life and death. You cultivate the ecstatic by placing trust in the present and its presences: by allowing it the space and time to show you something unanticipated. In this dissolution, a new, other self can emerge, one that temporarily inhabits another viewpoint. You are 'ec-static': outside of yourself.

You come here by letting go of things that connect you to your everyday world, the things that make you feel safe, as well as those that fill you with fear. The more you can temporarily forget what tethers you to daily life, the deeper you can go. The more you can unknow what you think you know, the weirder the questions that will ask themselves.

Where are you if you are outside of yourself? You merge with the intentions around you, which may have been invisible to you until that point. Something different and unpredictable simply shows itself: it is part of a reality that appears otherworldly, one most often hidden from view, yet inherent and belonging to the more-than-human world itself. This is why it matters where you do it, and with whom.

What is it like to experience something through human eyes as much as through a mushroom's sensorium? How do earth, rock and fungus draw?

How does a caterpillar see a butterfly? What is it like to live for thousands of years? To remember one's extraterrestrial origins?

You might be able to visit the same alien perspectives multiple times. These may give you the germ of your creative work, yet nothing objective can be said of them. Creative work is about learning to give form to these intuitions, while continuing to find ever deeper and stranger questions.

The intent to study is learning to let go of what preoccupies you, without discarding it, in favour of anything that might emerge. Temporarily forgetting what you think you know, is what allows you to move through any psychedelic session. Anything that comes can move through you. You may encounter questions that concern yourself, your friends and loved ones, dead or alive. Witnessing without engaging allows you to continue to reach further into ever newer and weirder perspectives. Let go of any and all of your questions and you might find the most interesting ones.

Note to *Who Is Asking the Questions Here?*

What do I know, when I am in this place, that I cannot know anywhere else? And what does this place know of me that I cannot know of myself? These are the two questions Robert MacFarlane asks any awe-inspiring landscape in *The Old Ways*. Here, this reversal of subjectivity is already a subtle offering up of oneself.

When performed as a psychedelic ritual involving substances, such an offering can come to feel anthrophagic: a spiritual kind of human consumption of the self. In *Time Is a Plant*, philosopher Michael Marder proposes that knowledge is the sublimation of digestion, and that this is already present in the activity of eating. Eating, he suggests, strives toward the unity of life and death, of life and knowledge.

Philosopher Thomas Nagel famously wrote of the unknowability of what it might be like to be a bat, or any other non-human being. The embrace of the ecstatic, however, turns unknowability to something like not-knowability: you can experience what it is like to be a bat, or a plant, or a mushroom, or a funny sticker on the fingernail of a child, but as you experience it, you are also not you anymore, and this experience doesn't produce the kind of knowledge sought by Nagel: I refer to this, elsewhere in this book, as non-knowledge.

Artists work with this weird kind of knowing. In his *Norton Lectures*, visual artist William Kentridge describes working in the studio as a series of irrational activities and ad-hoc decisions, followed by as much assiduity as possible. The artist in the studio needs to place trust in the physical: to allow it the space and time required for it to show something unanticipated.

Anthropologist, religious scholar and author Mircea Eliade held that revelations can appear in the mundane. You become aware of the sacred because it shows itself, as something completely different from the everyday, yet within an everyday context. You are confronted by a mysterious act of the manifestation of something of a completely different order, a reality that does not belong to our world, but is shown in objects that are an integral part of our natural, profane world. It can happen in anything you turn to, be it a tree or a stone, and when it happens, you are not worshiping the stone, or the tree itself, you're worshipping something entirely else showing itself through stone or tree – something undefinable, yet, as Eliade calls it, 'sacred'.

There are eerily similar petroglyph drawings in caves in the most distant places on Earth, from Tassili n'Ajjer in Algeria, and Fugoppe in Japan, to Nine Mile Canyon in Utah, to name but a few. One could speculate that, much as they have been produced by human individuals, another subjectivity is also at play, one that exists across deep time and far distances. Author John Berger reflects on this in *Portraits*, a splendid work on human visual culture across the centuries. Berger's deep insight was that we are witnessing in cave drawings two interconnected interior spaces. Produced in the darkness of the cave, the drawings we observe emerged as much from the interior of the Earth, as they do from that of the imagination. Using a bulge here, a hollow there, these drawings were created by the rock's surface as well as by the human mind and hand. In the case of the Tassili mushroom figures, which appear both humanoid and fungal, these suggest a state of being in which one may inhabit both forms simultaneously.

Image on p.52: Petroglyphs from Upper Yensi Basin, Khara-Chulum, Mongolia, and the Pegtymel rock art site, Chukot peninsula. *From Ekaterina Devlet and Marianna Devlet, 'Siberian Shamanistic Rock Art', in Adrzej Rozwadowski and Maria M. Kośk (eds.),* Spirits & Stones *(Poznán, Instytut Wschodni Uam, 2002), p. 126. Image reproduced with permission from Adrzej Rozwadowski.*

ALANG CI
S * KENYA
* KENYAL
CIRCUS *
BERAS

Caution, Care, Comfort

In many cultures, psychedelics are bound by strict rules about how to conduct daily life around them: in some cases, rules prescribe forms of fasting before, or sometimes after, a trip: abstinence from certain foods, alcohol, sexual intimacy, work or media use. In other contexts, it is recommended to eat a lot of meat before tripping, to build up strength. In certain rituals, psychedelics may not be taken alone – in others they have to be. While there is no set of rules that applies to every context, all study trips invite you to change many habitual comforts that, in our contemporary existence, can all too easily become unhealthy addictions. This is why you need to at least be aware of your own dietary and sexual habits, and to be able to change them if necessary.

There is a ground rule: asceticism makes psychedelics more powerful, whereas worldly attachments tend to ground you in material reality. Yet going too far with asceticism can become obstructive too, as you may not be able to integrate what you experience in a session back into your daily life. While psychedelics aren't physiologically addictive, anything can become addictive for the psyche. Your relationships with everything you are attached to define you, and they define your sessions. Your discipline in one directly translates into your capability with the other.

Eat the smoke and become ghost; drink the rare flower and become other; breathe the mushroom and let your eyes die. Some psychedelics will make you puke, shit, sweat, cramp, cry and feel like you are actually dying. Others will bring pure bliss. Both might happen within the same session. It may take days of slow surrender and deepening concentration, or merely a split second: you turn into nothing but streams of light, you merge with the intricate patterns of the world around you. And alongside a physical purging, a mental cleansing also plays out: any shame, fear or weakness becomes exposed. Study trips will not solve these problems. But if and when such things show up, you do get the chance to accept them, and perhaps even to relate to them differently.

Taken indoors, psychedelics will lead you towards introspection if you are alone, or group consciousness if you are together. Outdoors, they may strengthen your connection to the natural environment. But go deep enough, and there really is no longer any difference between inside and outside.

All this is not necessarily comfortable. Purification

and ecstasy go hand in hand, when preparing for a session, during one, or when integrating the experience. Over time you may learn and decide which kind of thoughtful abstinence will best prepare you for, and help you integrate, which particular kind of session. Some form of discomfort and fear might keep coming up before every session. This fear simply exposes your ego, that part of you that would prefer to remain in charge. This is not necessarily unhealthy, as it gives you an opportunity to face that fear. In that situation, you can permit any panic or anxiety to pass over and through you. When it has gone, only you will be left, with a clear path ahead.

Recognising patterns that are in the way becomes easy. Any projected longing towards anything supernatural – often superficially associated with psychedelics – can also be an obstacle. You get the opportunity to change patterns, too. Both psychedelics and creative work are always part of a discipline. Both activities cannot be forced. All you can do is to prepare your dedicated time and space, and accept that everything you did with your time until that point – what you read, did, ate, neglected, and how it affected your vital energies – will be influencing what may happen when, in ecstatic exchange, you surrender to your vitality.

Note to *Caution, Care, Comfort*

To 'become ghost' or to 'become other' are some of the ways in which Davi Kopenawa describes entering the psychedelic state in *The Falling Sky*. 'Surrendering to your vitality' is how philosopher Maurice Merleau-Ponty describes it in his *Phenomenology of Perception*.

To enter such a state brings up profound and often uncontrolled fear. My description of how to deal with fear is partly based on Frank Herbert's 'Litany against Fear' as it is offered in his science-fiction novel, *Dune*: 'I must not fear. Fear is the mind-killer. Fear is the little-death that brings total obliteration. I will face my fear. I will permit it to pass over me and through me. And when it has gone past I will turn the inner eye to see its path. Where the fear has gone there will be nothing. Only I will remain.'

Artist Marcos Kueh accompanies his work with descriptions that are remarkably open about his personal journey: 'Every living day is a personal pilgrimage to carry the cross of shame, so that one day I can maybe look like the uppers, talk like the uppers, think like the uppers, to exorcise the disgusting demon that I see in the mirror. But no matter how hard I try, I will always smell like desperation. [...] In silence, I split myself in half; dancing in between who I am and who I want to be.'

Kueh designs textile banners and combines them into awe-inspiring installations, where he blends the language of advertising campaigns with the oral storytelling practices from his home village. Kueh also calls his textile banners 'woven advertisements', and when you walk along them, they become the canopy of an urban jungle. 'What if Borneo, not New York, were the cultural epicentre of the world?', the artist asks.

Image on p.58: Marcos Kueh, Kenyalang Circus: Reconciliation, *2024. Industrial weaving, recycled PET, eight yarns, 300 × 300 × 50 cm. Photo: Cecília Coca, courtesy of Manifesta 15, Barcelona and Galerie Ron Mandos.*

Dosage, Duration, Danger

Psychedelic techniques of ecstasy are a technology – they are tools that enhance human capabilities for connection, inquiry, revelation, vision and study. As with any technology, there is a lot to learn and train, concerning practical aspects such as how much to take, how long to practice, and what to look out for.

First of all, no one but yourself can decide for you what to take or do – and an expert can only help you make your own decisions. Dosage is what makes the difference between medicine and toxin. If micro-dosing is prayer, a macrodose is mass, and a hero-dose is madness. Going too far once might 'cure' you from psychedelics for a long time, your life slowly catching up to what was revealed to you.

There are thresholds of lower and upper limits in dosage – or depth and duration if we're talking about techniques. These are different for everyone, and related to the type and strength of your everyday habits. Noting down what you take, how you take it, how much, for how long, with whom; and afterwards, what you have observed and how intensely it has manifested itself: these are activities that, in themselves, can help an improvised psychedelic event turn in the direction of a study trip. It will also allow you to compare previous and future sessions.

But focusing too much on technicalities is itself an obsession that can distract from any real inquiry. You can time your practice, but you can also choose to time yourself, as part of your study.

The act of measuring your dosage also affects the trip. For a study trip, you may be measuring, but once you're in it, you are also being measured. You become the material that other entities – known or unknown – are studying, too. That's why, after enough measurements, you'll be ready to let your substance tell you how much you need, or let your practice tell you how long it should last. As with any painter, sculptor, designer or woodworker, the ambition is to become so well acquainted with the material that it becomes an extension of yourself, telling you wordlessly what you need to know.

There are also contra-indications: any technique or substance that threatens your abilities to function in everyday life – outside of the study trip itself – is unhelpful. Start small, and seek guidance, if not company. Make sure you're in good physical and mental health. A healthy mind is able to integrate what comes up through psychedelics, whether from the subconscious or the 'over-conscious'.

Subtle psychedelics such as microdosing – as well as mindfulness techniques – have become popular ways to enhance daily life and work. A longer period of microdosing might be considered a thinly stretched macrodose, slowly facilitating similar inner study.

Coming back from a study trip is as important as going into it. For those who are sensitive to psychosis, psychedelics may not be suitable at all, but practicing the return may still be relevant. The aesthetic elements of ceremony – rhythm, expression, movement, speech, poetry – can help, as does creative work during everyday life.

Here, creativity and psychedelics align: a rule of thumb is to have every technical step you take – methodical, measured, engineered and outward – be accompanied by a magical step, magical in the sense that it is informed by what seems to come from within, from beyond the senses. Use a tool and then make sure to also work by hand; take a substance, and the next time try a technique; go a bit deeper than last time, and after that take or do nothing at all. These are similar movements in different directions. Practicing both allows for contextualisation and reciprocity. Allow every action its own countermovement of non-action; rest more than you do not rest.

Your surroundings morph into another world, with every object seemingly folding itself inside out. Everything around you is both vitally alive and dead and both at once. A chair shows itself to be made of human bones, adorned with floral details. What if artworks aren't made or constructed, but living things that grow?

Note to *Dosage, Duration, Danger*

'Rest, more than you do not rest' is a quote from James Jealous's treatise on osteopathy, *An Osteopathic Odyssey*. In this book, Jealous stresses the importance of stillness, something that can be equally applied to practices of psychedelic study.

Mind and body must be in balance to achieve an 'over-mind consciousness' that is normal and sane, according to poet H.D. She experienced over-mind as an aqueous cap that covers the head, blurring her vision. 'Transparent, fluid yet with definite body, like a closed sea-plant, jelly-fish or anemone.' In her writing, anyone can cultivate this over-mind, as long as they stimulate the other manifestations of life: the body must feel desire, and be open to pleasure, the mind must be alive with intellectual inquisitiveness.

In the old tradition of *Taoist Yoga*, as described by Charles Luk, such an egress happens through specific meditations, and a lot of care is involved. One should only be allowed to leave the physical body in fine weather, for instance, and only for a short time. This practice should only be undertaken during daytime, and initially only weekly. Only with time, he suggests, might this frequency intensify.

Where substances are involved, a lot of advice about plant medicine can be found in Dale Pendell's *Pharmako* books, a multi-volume encyclopaedia dedicated to the literary roots of plant medicine. The line on the difference between medicine and toxin, can be found there.

A particular attitude towards care and balance is exemplified by Tadeas Podracky's *Morana Chair*. Podracky bases the design on themes of death and rebirth and the presence of bones and flowers, both found in folk rituals. But the final shape of the work emerges through the process of long hours of craft. In an email, Podracky clarified: 'I was inspired by the hybridization process of folk rituals. In Czech culture, we have traditions like the drowning of

Morana [or puppets of a Pagan goddess].' These folk rituals survive by being transformed and reinvented in contemporary, suburban areas, in a living cycle of cultural adaptation. The objects used in the rituals, through personification and anthropomorphism, turn into more than just tools. In other words, non-living things become animated through myth and ritual. The *Morana Chair*, too, was made with a mythological function in mind first: not following a modernist idea of function, nor a post-modern notion of decoration – but as an object that in its use opens another kind of perception, rooted in a reinvented mythology.

Image on p.64: Tadeas Podracky, Morana, *2024. White waxed spruce wood, 183 x 63 x 69 cm. Photo: Eva Rybarova, courtesy of the artist.*

1.b.
1.a.
2.
3.
4.
5.
6.
plastico, alambre, tela
EJEMPLAR HERBARIO
RECOLECTOR
LUGAR
FECHA
10 april 2018
Expedición Sicilia

The Need for Roots

Do you know the organisms that facilitate your trips? Psychedelic study encourages different ways of knowing, but before you can take this any further, you may wish to become acquainted with all the actors involved.

Before a trip on a substance, ask yourself what you know of its context. Where and how did it grow, or how was it produced? Which communities – human and more-than-human – did it pass through on its way to you? Who made money off of it? Some psychedelic substances are legal in one country and illegal in another. Do you know which are native to your landscape?

Everything you find out about the substance's provenance, life and story, influences the trip. By extension, the choice to ignore all of this may impoverish the outcomes. Contextual information allows you to recognise what you encounter in your trip more effectively, allowing you to deal with it more confidently, and to journey deeper. A study trip with an awareness of contextual relations can foster responsibility and reciprocity, both of which are fundamental to unfolding its full potential.

In urbanised centres, food, water, energy, information and waste come and go through complex and opaque industrialised systems. This facilitates a comfortable life, but has also severed connections with local and indigenous knowledge, knowledge that is possibly irretrievably lost, because the landscape that held it has been irrevocably transformed.

The resulting alienation is also psychological: many phenomena experienced through psychedelics are only interpreted as fantasy. Daily life can be so estranged, that any paradisical experience can only be an illusion: something to be found in an afterlife, or at best in a dream.

Growing, finding, or making your own substances, or learning about and from others that do, helps to reconnect. This involves finding friends: a community of people, human and more-than-human, who share an interest with you. In fact, you're finding out what it means to reconnect to your sense of place.

A synthetic substance may need more contextualisation than a purely organic one, owing to the alienated context of its production; a cultivated substance, in turn, may need more than one that grows in the wild. The extra work of contextualising – if you're willing and able to do it – might make a synthetic substance into an interesting choice.

When psychedelic substances are prohibited, for instance for safety reasons, that prohibition also forecloses the possibility of asking those difficult, critical, perhaps even subversive questions that study trips often bring up. Instead of prohibition, can we imagine non-commercial, non-dogmatic, non-institutionalised, collectively and creatively organised psychedelic guidance?

The work of recontextualisation is equally important for creative work: any outcome can be open to others who suffer from similar estrangements. In its own way, such work can fulfil a contemporary shamanic function: the expression of a need for reconnection.

People have performed study trips in every time period and on every continent, in infinitely different ways. Imagine it all happening simultaneously, in the same space. Fragments, snippets of rituals from the world over, around you. You're enveloped in waves of visuals and sound, a shifting tapestry of sensory stimuli. A tree speaking in colours. Factoryscapes where every breath was built and made possible by the countless deaths of others. You have a sense of being part of something larger. You become aware of how your own sessions are both direct extensions, and reinventions, of the infinite ways in which people, ancient and contemporary, have studied through psychedelics. A psychedelic study trip that is newly in touch with traditional, ecological knowledge isn't afraid to face new, hybrid contemporary spirits emerging from strange new landscapes.

Note to *The Need for Roots*

The Need for Roots is the title of a book by Simone Weil, in which she describes rootedness as the most important and least recognised need of the human soul. Rootedness is the opposite of uprootedness, or the alienation caused by industrialisation and colonialism. Rootedness comes from having a stable sense of belonging to a place and a community.

Philosopher David Abram writes (in *The Spell of the Sensuous*) how for writing-based people it is difficult to approach the vividness and intensity which becomes legible to communities more reliant on oral transmission. Abram writes about the effect of prolonged and isolated stays in nature: the part of our selves reliant on written language becomes dysfunctional; what remains is another way of sensing, one that is closer to that brought about by psychedelics.

The problem of contextualisation is not only valid for psychedelics. Tobacco is an example of a substance considered sacred in many cultures, and only to be used in ritual ways, not in commodified and consumerist ones. Similarly, cocaine as it is most well known is the tragic by-product of a profound de-contextualisation – a toxic, globalised commodity instead of a sacred plant rooted in landscape and ritual. A far older, contextualised, healthy, non-addictive and medicinal practice remains largely unacknowledged.

Alberto Baraya is the artist behind the *Artificial Plant Herbarium*, an ongoing project of artistic taxonomy, and a project that 're-roots'. During various expeditions in Europe, Latin America and elsewhere, Baraya visits communities, and collects samples of artificial flowers, studying the ways in which they have been used, often in religion and ceremony. In this detail from a page from the Sicilian herbarium, we see a 'Jasmine Provenzano (made in China)', found on a grave.

Image on p.70: Alberto Baraya, 'Provenzano jasmin, pl. 39. / Collector: a.baraya / Place: Corleone / Date: 10 April 2018. Dimensions: 60 x 40 x 4,3 cm. Found object, fabric, wire and plastic (made in China)'. From A Sicilian Expedition: New Herbs from Palermo and Surroundings. *Alberto Baraya,* Herbario de plantas artificiales, *Manifesta 18, Palermo, 2018. Courtesy of the artist.*

Through the Portal

The first thing people associate with psychedelics are strange patterns and vibrant colours. These rich visuals are the start: the famous doors of perception, through which a study trip will be taking you. This doorway is a world of ornament. When it is made with dedication, skill, and joy, ornament is vital: it shows the way to, and makes space for, transition.

Maybe you don't actually see a door; maybe, at first, you fly over a distant cityscape; through floating snowflakes and swirling flowers; a giant hall populated by cartoon-like clowns, weird aliens, a multi-tentacled, laughing insectoid. You may be moving through a membrane of thoughts and feelings, attending to each of your three, five, or six, energetically different bodies, depending on which tradition you turn to. All around you buzzes with patterns of all shapes, sizes and colours, folding in and out of each other, taking your worldly surroundings away with them. These are the living inscriptions on the gate. You are now fully inside ornament. This doorway is depicted in the art of many different cultures. It's quite something: the gate where the psychedelic and the everyday transition into each other; where the sacred and the profane touch.

And it may stop there: as long as you're looking for kicks, you will not go further. You will be provided with an infinite scroll in multiple dimensions. In time, the psychedelic world may start to become a brutal, violent, distracting, impenetrable circus. But it is in fact only benevolently keeping you away from what you are not yet ready to witness, what is quite literally beyond your imagination.

Enjoy the visuals, but don't engage, don't let yourself be distracted. Follow what the visuals transition into. At some point, maybe you won't even notice them anymore. Remaining undistracted, and looking not at, but seeing through, the spectacle: this is how you can surrender to the experience and its learnings. A tube-like tunnel, an enormous spaciousness, or a feeling of elevation, takes you further into a world of light.

Study trips can help open blockages caused by a devotion to possessions, status, and appearances. Like in the making of ornament itself, it is your dedication, skill and joy that are vital, as you find and align with the intent to study. Beyond the portal, everything is weirdly mirrored: the stage has always already been set by all your previous actions. With every visit, this strange other world becomes increasingly familiar, without losing any of its strangeness. Returning to it is not about attaining self-realisation or finding happiness. It's the beginning of asking the right questions for you and yours.

Psychedelics are an ornament in time and space, an entirely superfluous efflorescence unnecessary to worldly life: they do the opposite of all efforts to plan and shape the world; they are a ritual that marks transitions towards surrender, devotion and celebration.

In some communities, psychedelic substances are always available, for anyone to take. In others, they are guarded with secrecy, laced with taboo and prohibition, and are only occasionally available in the margins, or to an elite. What an individual study trip is to you, might be considered sacred by your community. Because psychedelics can be disruptive to everyday life, they need safe boundaries. May you be lucky enough, responsible, and able in equal measure to set such boundaries yourself. The ornamental portal might turn out to be no more than a small garden gate.

Note to *Through the Portal*

'Flying snow and falling flowers' is an image offered by Charles Luk in *Taoist Yoga* to describe a particular set of visual patterns you can access through meditation, and as a way of experiencing what I like to call 'the ornamental portal'. Such a doorway is much more physical, and much more integrated in more secular societies, than you might think. There are portals everywhere, ornamental thresholds – whether in sacred spaces, bureaucratic buildings or technological processes. These are doors of perception, too: we are reminded of Aldous Huxley's famous text on psychedelics, titled after a passage by William Blake: 'If the doors of perception were cleansed every thing would appear to man as it is, Infinite. For man has closed himself up, till he sees all things thro' narrow chinks of his cavern.'

What I call 'access to the sacred' in this text is closely related to what Jim Corbett described as 'sabbath'. Living in wilderness, Corbett followed the lunar month and spent celebratory nights under the starry sky as ways of accessing the sacred, which he referred to as 'Eden's Gate'.

Artists Gijs Frieling and Job Wouters, known together as FreelingWaters, paint onto a variety of surfaces, from walls to books, clothing, antique cabinets and coffins. Their painting and calligraphy is sometimes abstract, sometimes figurative: animals, plants, or the textures of marble and wood. Wouters calls their writing-like animal and object shapes 'figurative writing'. The ancient yet highly refined manual crafts involved are a welcome exception in an increasingly automated world. Every peculiarity in their hand movements translates directly into a unique shape. In the trance of the painter-writer as they conjure a world, I see a process that echoes the earliest cave paintings, tens of thousands of years ago. These objects are as much the result of joy and concentration as of incantation, giving their work its dazzling attraction and synaesthetic quality. A fingerprint becomes a fish eye, a blot becomes a stone.

Synaesthesia, or the overlap and blending of the senses is, according to David Abram, the capability to remember an older, preconceptual way of sensing. This is accessible to anyone willing to surrender to the natural environment, or to an artwork.

While FreelingWaters' hand-painted, wooden cabinets are held in collections and museums all over the world, some of their cabinets are flat, and exist only as a trompe-l'oeil painting on a wall. As is the case for the painting reproduced in this book, these doors are for perception and perception alone.

Image on p.76: FreelingWaters, Flat Cabinet, *2025. Mural painting. Installation at Bunker23, Tartsch, South Tyrol. Courtesy of the artists.*

Part II: Celebration

The White Light of the Beginning

White light pushes away a swirling cacophony of brightly coloured forms; you had let it all come over you, and now you let it go, following white light. There is no more clamour, distraction, or seduction, just peace. You're in a crystal chamber: a space without objects, expanding into infinity; in the flaming white pearl of the great maker; in the foamy spring of vital energy; in all-encompassing, unconditional love. Supernatural light pervades your limbs; splendour shines not just around or above you, but throughout your heart and lungs. It's the most intense experience possible: the mind containing all objects, situations, thoughts, and feelings, of everyone and everything, everywhere and of all times, a supernova exploding silently in the middle of your head. You're inside a white hole, where time and space fuse, a singularity, a white-out. Here, loving others and acquiring knowledge are clearly all that matters, independently of dogma or ideology. Without worrying whether there will be life for you after death, you experience eternity and gratitude.

You may have encountered the clear, white light of the beginning without having ever touched psychedelics. Or perhaps, you've been experimenting with psychedelics for years, and still have never been anywhere near such a place. Many wisdom traditions recognise the experience of a white light, and while it is a clear marker of specific psychedelic substances, it can also occur through the long and dedicated discipline of techniques. Other times, the white light may meet you unexpectedly, unprompted.

It is an otherworldly place, utterly weird. Yet it feels familiar. It may be the house of your unconscious – or your over-conscious – a home you might have forgotten you had. And, just as a home you haven't been to in a while, it might need some care.

The creation of this light may happen when you learn to shift your attention from one field of consciousness to another. In physiological terms, this means: when you do everything you can to attend to your physical, mental and social wellbeing, and then you let go of it all, allowing your nervous system to do the rest. This is your innate capacity to allow your everyday, active awareness to be witnessed by a second, observing, non-acting consciousness.

It can happen during meditation too: attention turns in on itself, while everything from the outer world melts away. You can cultivate it, moving one step deeper every time. In more ways than one, this movement is similar to taking a step back from creative work: you stop, and witness what was made. You gain an overview. And when you return to making, you may have gained a new trust about where to go next. You are holding space for the mystery of something you allow yourself not to know. With the arrival of the white light, the work becomes about embracing the dark, the inscrutable.

Seemingly simple creative operations like this may very well be unplanned, but you can continue to fine-tune them. In the long term, they can grow unpredictable results. A mandala can spirit forth an experience that is unfathomable, unknowable, yet its making is a sequence of simple, repeated steps. Its resulting, complex form documents the process by which you have let go of trying to resolve complexity.

However you find and experience this switch between light and darkness, it is a marker of study. The clear light of the beginning is no singular moment, and no end goal, neither physiologically nor metaphorically. That is to say that you cannot expect enlightenment, and even if that were available, it would not be about you, but rather a manifestation of the vitality and presence of everything around you, that you might have never noticed before.

Once you have given new life to this home of white light, you will know you can find your way back to it, in many different ways. And when you do return, it will be a place that you can invite others into: a home for new questions, presences and ways of being that are making themselves known to you.

Note to *The White Light of the Beginning*

In this chapter, I refer to the white light as a kind of home. Davi Kopenawa speaks about constructing such a home. Young shamans train to construct their own 'malokka', an Amazonian Indigenous house, in that otherworldly realm while under the influence, and invite into the process only those spirits they want to work with.

But such construction is not an active, worldly action. It is rather a letting go, something I will return to later, in the chapter *To Do and Not to Do*.

In a conversation with Lucia Pietroiusti for the catalogue of his 2025 exhibition, *WITNESS*, Antony Gormley describes 'a room without objects… the space inside the body that you have to be incredibly still to access'.

In *The Taoist Body*, scholar Kristofer Schipper describes a state of mind in which all calculating thoughts have vanished. He calls it, 'to know the white', which is followed by another movement, that of 'keeping the black'. Schipper proposes that our contemporary obsession with unlimited knowledge makes us lose sight not only of the very real limits of human abilities, but also of the obscurity in which all sources of being lie. It is from this obscurity, this not-knowing, that springs 'pure whiteness', the 'flaming pearl of vital energy'.

For Mircea Eliade, over the course of human history, there have been a thousand different ways of translating this spiritual moment into language: 'The meaning of the light is, on the one hand, ultimately a personal discovery and, on the other, each man discovers what he was spiritually and culturally prepared to discover. Whatever his previous ideological conditioning, a meeting with the light produces a break in the subject's existence, revealing to him – or making clearer than before the world of the spirit, of holiness and of freedom.'

Artist Harm van den Dorpel programmed a wall-mounted piece whose result he called

Creation of Light. The pixelated artwork, engraved in metal with light, is the output of coding, testing and tweaking: when undertaken with a specific mindset, this can be a form of meditation. The image is not planned, nor intentionally composed. Rather, it appeared out of a series of several programmatic, algorithmic and mental processes.

In a conversation with writer William Kherbek, Van den Dorpel likens this work to a mandala. In a mandala, the visual result obtained is only a part of the work: the process it takes to create it, and that of observing it carefully, are just as integral to it. Working through simple steps and techniques generates a work of magic: there are no ideological givens, no pre-ordained messages in the work. All of its signs remain open.

Image on p.84: Harm van den Dorpel, Creation of Light*, 2024. Wall object, photographic exposure on metallic paper, 100 × 100 cm. Courtesy of the artist.*

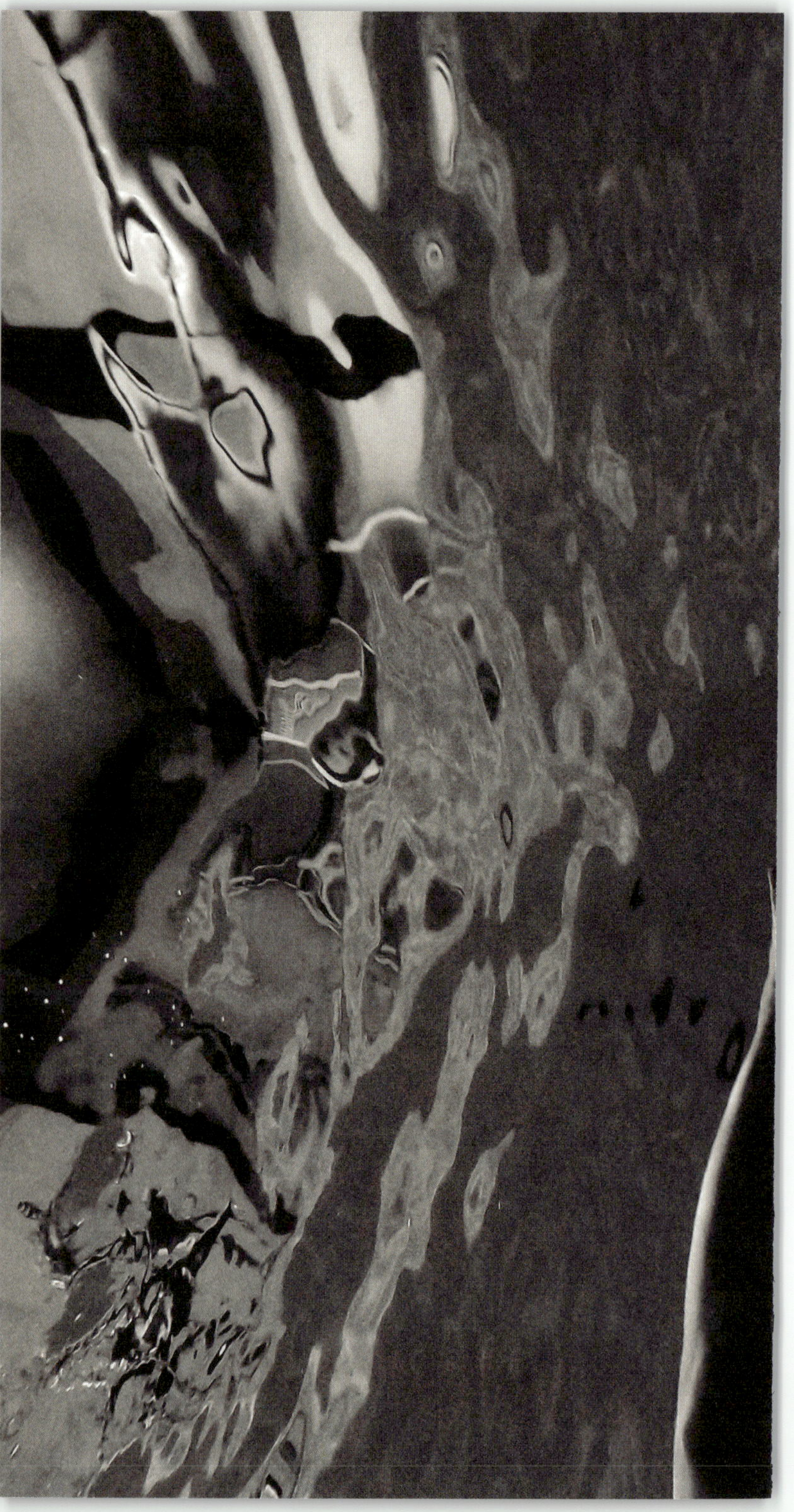

Navigating Psychedelic Spacetime

Whether you are alone in nature, singing in a sauna, repeating the words of holy scripture, taking medicinal psychoactive substances, sitting in a dark cave for days, floating in a saltwater tank, praying fervently, or surrendering to masterfully crafted artwork; whether it's beats or breaths, particles or waves, an infinitesimally small moment, or an extended period of time; a certain resonance dissolves your ego, and merges you with your surroundings.

This heightened state of ecstatic awareness has been called by many names: over-mind, over-soul, more-than-human consciousness, the view from nowhere. Some describe it as a particular place, just outside of time: hyperspace, the dreaming, the mundus imaginalis, the upside-down, the elsewhere, the otherwise, the above-below, the field, the manifesting. While with every label another nuance is added, no description can define it. Where is it, even? Is this an unthinkable place nested within your own mind? Is this the imagination? Are you going mad? Are you navigating a spiritual, immaterial world? Or is this something else, a space literally in-between, one that is there all the time, yet that you cannot usually see? Have you then simply, suddenly, become aware of all the invisible particles, energies and flows that connect you to everything else?

If you're still surrounded by human people in this place, by now they have become pure, fluid intention. It's full here: there are other, vital presences, ones you know and ones you didn't know you knew. All contradictions are lifted, space and time are one. You're enveloped by a sea-plant, a jellyfish, a forest, a cosmic hall, a cathedral. Your awareness is heightened and notices both negative and positive ideas and apparitions. Some people find ancestors and descendants here, tree spirits, ideas as alive as you and me.

It doesn't matter anymore how you got here, or what belief system has brought you here. Perhaps you remember this place from distant childhood memories. You may realise that this is the world as it always has been.

Is this where artists come to when they work? Is this what they reach, and then try to translate into the sensible realm? If so, then they are met with boundless possibility, because this is a place that is always changing. And yet, there isn't a single thing you can really 'do' here, in the conventional sense. Your awareness is still here, but everything, including your body, your whole person, has become dream-like. You're not dreaming, but you're not awake either. Here, logic fails, and dreaming and waking are distinctions that make no sense anymore.

So why are you back here now? Can you pick up where you left off? What is present now in this home of light? What are you encountering, even if you might not understand it, that you might bring back into the tangible world?

After all this talk of intention and attention, here is where you practice it: every time more confidently, recognising when you are practicing the fullest and most absolute attention, and when you are not. Each time, you are shedding something else that keeps your attention away from your simple observation and presence in this luminous home. As attachments, worries, anxieties, desires and ambitions fall away, what deeper contemplation arises? What can you witness, manifesting around you?

Remember, memory is a similar process to imagination, even if it appears to move in a different direction. This world of intention will imprint itself upon your memory and stretch your imagination. If this were it, this would already be enough.

Note to *Navigating Psychedelic Spacetime*

'Weird things happen when humans try to cast off the shackles of linear time and assume the vantage of eternity,' writes Meghan O'Gieblyn (in her essay 'The Trouble with Reality' in *The New York Review of Books*), referring to Boethius's *On the Consolation of Philosophy*. Rational understanding here does not suffice. 'That purely transcendent, objective vantage outside the totality of things. Spinoza called it "sub specie aeternitatis". Hannah Arendt named it "the Archimedean point".'

In this chapter, I am borrowing from several additional descriptions of this place, from poet H.D., writer Ralph Waldo Emerson, Sufism scholar Henri Corbin, psychedelics evangelist Terence McKenna, artist Doreen Reid Namakarra, the Bhagavad Gita, as well as philosophers Michael Marder and David Abram.

In several of his works, philosopher Vilém Flusser suggests that such a state may be reached 'telematically', or through technology. In *Into the Universe of Technical Images*, a book that remains profoundly ambivalent about the rise of technological mediation, he describes this state, when reached through technical means, as orgasmic, while simultaneously admitting to being happy he won't live to see it.

Revital Cohen & Tuur van Balen's *Heavens* is such a 'telematic' work. The video still in this chapter comes from an immersive installation, in which the film is projected onto a domed ceiling. The work explores a scientific hypothesis according to which the octopus evolved from a squid infected by a virus that originated in outer space. The work departs from this while also acknowledging, following Walter Benjamin, that the development of astronomical technology has brought about the death of the cosmic experience. As Lucia Pietroiusti writes: 'The more we see, the less we sense; the more we know, the less we conceive.' The film, and libretto, are both paced in accordance with the emotional pace of a Catholic mass. They work their way from this potential cosmic origin to a vaster, cosmic state, in which interconnection becomes ubiquitous. The traditional rules of film don't apply here: there is no fixed orientation to watch it, no beginning nor end. Surrendering to the work opens questions and movements between human and more-than-human consciousness.

Image on p.90: Revital Cohen & Tuur Van Balen, Heavens, *2021 (still). Video installation, 30'. Courtesy of the artists.*

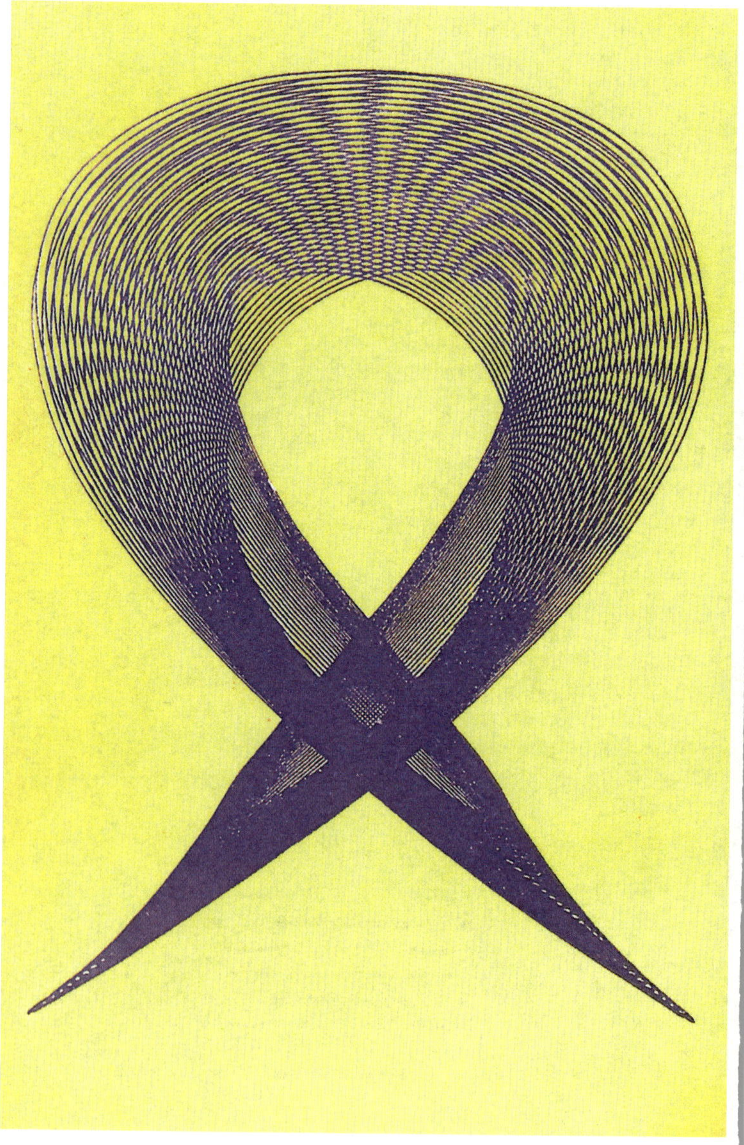

To Do and Not to Do

Is an image alive? Or a thought? When you have an image in mind, is it also a thought? Image-thoughts certainly have lifespans, and the same thought can come up in different people. Images can be vital, viral, and they can go extinct. How does it feel to hold a particular thought-image in mind? Can you invite an older one back? Can you hold in your mind the same image-thoughts as those of the people around you? If image-thoughts are things, can you let go of some, and engage with others?

What if what you are imagining-thinking moves about in space? What if what you feel-see-think is a wave that washes the shores of other bodies, becoming part of them, like music? What if thought-images grow verdant shoots from under your feet, connecting you to others, growing and blossoming? What if the aspiration to enfold all presented itself as a living, purple, shimmering embrace in yellow light? You may witness a world of vibrations, a swarm of fleeting micro-events, playing out on a cosmic scale. Porous image-thoughts, mental objects with life cycles of their own, merging with you and others, transforming you, attracting further thought-images.

What is a thought-form to an idea, a metaphor, an archetype, a spirit? Watching, holding, being present with an image-thought can be confronting, scary, beautiful. Psychedelics turn you over to streams of image-thoughts, and there is nothing you can do about it.

This is precisely the point: not-doing. Non-action is not the same as no action. It is still action, but effortless. It is not the same as doing nothing, taking it easy, or evading difficulty. You go with the flow in effortless non-action: the flow might take you through terrifying territory and demand extreme attention. Being able to refrain from immediately responding to all those things that present themselves is sometimes called 'ego death'. This may be a somewhat inaccurate term, because it is something that happens all the time, and not just once; just like the regeneration of life – and the re-establishment of the ego – also happens over and over.

Such non-action can be trained, but not through any active effort. With every psychedelic session, this capability becomes more agile. The discipline here lies simply in the commitment to continue learning, to turn the fullest attention towards something truly vast. With every attempt, it becomes easier to reach this state of mind and body, because you will start to recognise it.

Learning to do this in the field of psychedelics helps you do it in the field of creativity, too. Creativity engages as much with material forms as with immaterial ones – a painted rainbow is simultaneously concrete and abstract. It resonates with sometimes visible, sometimes invisible image-thoughts, in both maker and audience. It is always an act of the imagination. Such work cannot be forced into being. All active actions are only conditional: clearing out your schedule, emptying your desk, emptying your mind, putting pen to paper or brush to canvas. And then allowing yourself to be light in effortless non-action: this is part of every creative session.

What's more, you might have the sense that any creative project you work on grows and changes, even when you're not working on it. It's the pause in the music; tree roots growing invisibly in early spring. After a walk, a rest, a night, a season, your work will look different to you. Ideas will have ripened, new subconscious connections will have been forged: all this happens in non-action.

Note to *To Do and Not to Do*

'Non-action' is how the Taoist concept of 'wu-wei' is sometimes translated. This was made famous by Lao Tzu: 'the sage takes no action and yet nothing is left undone'.

Non-action is also closely related to the negative capability made famous by the poet John Keats, who in a letter describes being 'capable of being in uncertainties, Mysteries, doubts, without any irritable reaching after fact and reason.'

Simone Weil uses the terms 'non-acting action' when she describes 'prayer in the soul': 'The attention turned with love towards God (or in a lesser degree, towards anything which is truly beautiful) makes certain things impossible for us.' Focusing your attention is a different kind of action, a non-acting action.

Annie Besant's drawing is one of a series of 'thought-forms', works that are simultaneously abstract and concrete. They represent visual and graphic patterns, while also giving shape to one single, particular thought. Annie Besant and C.W. Leadbeater explain the making of the images: one person would be sitting in meditation and would try to fill their mind with a particular thought, while another, making intangible contact, would attempt to 'see' the visual forms of these thoughts as they took shape in their own mind.

This particular thought-form was connected with 'the aspiration to enfold all mankind in order to draw them upwards towards the high ideal which shone so clearly before their eyes'.

It seems impossible that any technique would yield more than a static representation of an ever-changing, multi-faceted, multi-dimensional, richly textured and fleeting thought-form. However, this is one of the earliest examples of modern, Western, abstract art. Here, non-action is precisely the kind of action that is required to allow these forms to take shape. Besant and Leadbeater's publication, *Thought Forms*, is now in the public domain. Curator Carolyn Christov-Bakargiev calls *Thought Forms* one of the first examples of modern abstract art theory (in her introduction for the catalogue of the 14th Istanbul Biennial, *SALT-WATER: A Theory of Thought Forms*). She calls these thought-forms 'embodied entities of the imaginal realm'. And: 'They are forms of the real world that can be apprehended in intense states of awareness, meditation or attention.'

Image on p.96: Annie Besant and C.W. Leadbeater, An Aspiration to Enfold All. *Machine drawing, from Thought-Forms (Bradford: Percy Lund, Humphries & Co. Ltd., 1901), p. 66. Reproduction in public domain.*

Bliss Trip, Study Trip

In the centre of your centre, under your navel, you may feel warmth, as the psychedelic state excites your body, and as your excitement turns into vitality. Tingling sensations may rise up inside you, reaching the crown of your head, and even further up, somewhere above you. The world around you may have been inert to you before, but now it is clearly lively, and you're in touch with it. Your surroundings engage you, become you, interactively, in intercourse.

An angel fills your heart, licking your skull gently from the inside, ejaculating pink clouds into your being. A rainbow radiates from your chest. You're a flower of spiritual energy, grown in a cosmic garden. Golden arrows of light penetrate your body. A planet-size lover holds you, you feel your every nerve cell quiver in orgiastic creativity.

How can a thousand-year-orgasm, uniquely yours, be good for anyone else as well? You have reached a state of pure love towards ideas, people, artworks, natural entities – and this sensation has not asked of you to have any physical relations at all. Energy can take on a character of mind. You see, not only with your eyes. You see, and feel, with every nerve and cell of your body, with your gut, your spine. This is womb-vision, full-body-vision. From this place, you may become capable of seeing others in their entire being, too: to know them, and not just in the way they choose to present themselves. This seeing, this new weird kind of knowing, is a form of being in communion. It's a miraculous experience, worthy of the most exquisite marble, accessible to everyone, in many ways and through an infinite number of substances or techniques.

Some traditions call for sexual abstinence before a psychedelic session, while others prescribe celibacy for a period afterwards. Sexual abstinence can work to your advantage, giving you stronger, deeper, and at the same time lighter, trips. But it only works if it is freely cultivated, not if it is self-imposed. And more than your own worldly actions regarding sexuality, it is your attitude towards those actions that counts. When you make love, can you dedicate the energy you are generating not just to yourself and your lover, but also to the liveliness of what surrounds you? When in an ecstatic session, as energies are exchanged and emotions entangled, can you learn to look inwards and discern which boundaries to maintain, and which to dissolve?

Bliss may happen where there is harmony: if you can recognise and accept boundaries, acknowledge desires, follow up only on dedicated, loving intentions. All of your smallest erotic deliberations and decisions throughout everyday life – the lightest fantasies and darkest repressions – have already set the stage. Being able to recognise and let go of distractions from the outside, as well as urges from the inside: these are key mental capacities that will allow ecstasy to flow through your entire being, uniting sexuality, vitality and spirituality.

Ecstatic bliss is always available in the making of art. Whenever you find yourself bored, listless, nerve-wrackingly insecure, remember that through all the hard work that is creative labour, at the peak of inspired creation, a type of erotic rapture will find you. What if psychedelic bliss is just that: being present with creative germination, so that you may nurture it?

Even looking at a work by someone else may induce it. Works that express an ecstatic state – be it a sculpture in a church, or a poem by a medieval mystic – already provide you with an exercise for their recipient: you are being called on to reflect upon your own relationship to the erotic. This looking out, combined with a willingness and the ability to look in, is already part of the journey.

After a bliss trip, you'll be satisfied, but not depleted. You will feel it staying with you, somewhere in the background of your everyday life.

Note to
Bliss Trip, Study Trip

Poet H.D. uses the words 'love-region', 'womb-vision', and 'genital-vision' when she describes a feeling of physical warmth and heightened state of awareness. For H.D., this state could be triggered without touch, substance or technique.

Knowing someone or something finds intimate expression in sexual union, according to Jim Corbett, who writes (in *Goatwalking*): 'Sexual love is the aspect of one's intercourse with the Creation's kaleidoscopic personal presence that usually awakens human beings to full awareness of another's presence, even when most of the world still seems to be composed of mere objects.' Sexual love is an inseparable aspect of communion, he writes elsewhere. And: 'To see how sexual love illustrates communion is to see that the personal intercourse of one person with another coheres by virtue of the Presence for Whom there is no other; only in this unity can one person know another, presence-to-presence.'

Mystical texts describe these states of ecstatic union beautifully. The anonymous medieval text *The Cloud of Unknowing* can even be read as a kind of instruction manual for meditation and prayer.

Baroque sculptor and architect Gianlorenzo Bernini famously represented this bliss, the ecstasy of religious awakening, as a flaming golden arrow that pierces the heart of Saint Teresa. 'A combination of infinite pain and utter pleasure, the pain of dying, of letting the world go, of disappearing into the clouds, and the simultaneous pleasure of being nothing but the love of god.' I cite Carolyn Christov-Bakargiev (in her essay 'Double Vision' in the catalogue for the exhibition *Ecstasy* at LA MoCA): 'The angel is portrayed more physical than the saint, the angel is a worldly being, a kind of displaced self-portrait of the artist, observing ecstasy from the outside and conjuring up the statue from the rock.'

Saint Teresa of Avila's own writings are themselves sometimes a kind of trip report. In the *Meditations on the Song of Songs* she writes: 'Now, my Lord, I ask you nothing else in this life but to kiss me with the kiss of your mouth, and this in such a way that I should not be able, even though I wished, to withdraw myself from this union and friendship.'

Image on p.102: Gianlorenzo Bernini, The Ecstasy of Saint Teresa, *1647-52. Marble. Rome, Chiesa di Santa Maria della Vittoria.*

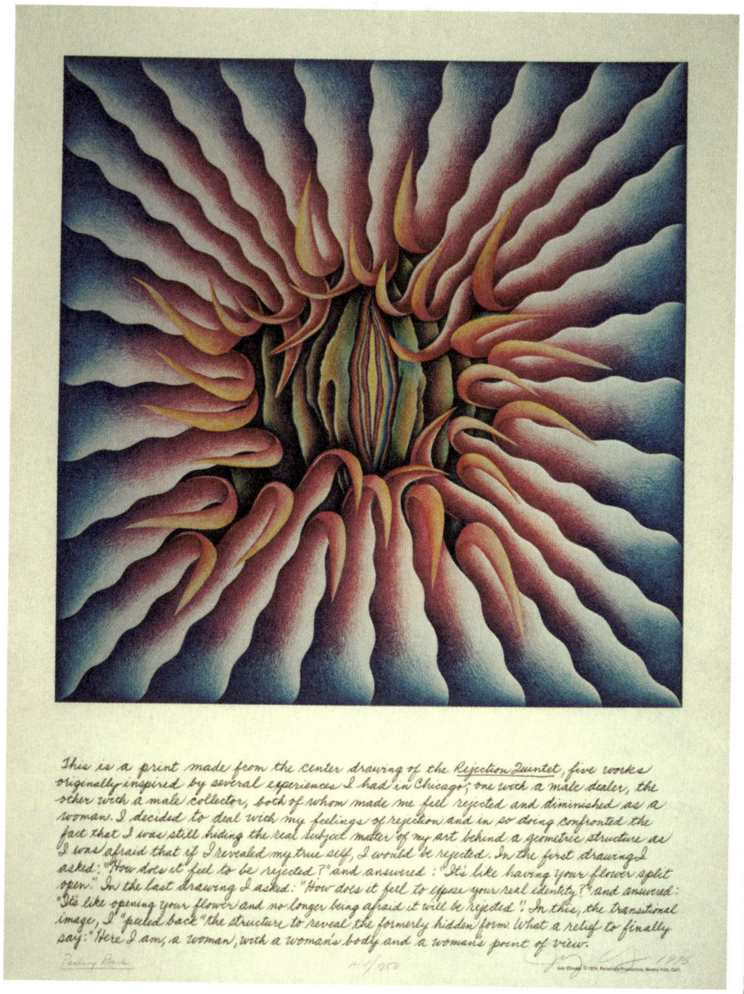
This is a print made from the center drawing of the Rejection Quintet, five works originally inspired by several experiences I had in Chicago; one with a male dealer, the other with a male collector, both of whom made me feel rejected and diminished as a woman. I decided to deal with my feelings of rejection and in so doing confronted the fact that I was still hiding the real subject matter of my art behind a geometric structure as I was afraid that if I revealed my true self, I would be rejected. In the first drawing I asked: "How does it feel to be rejected?" and answered: "It's like having your flower split open." In the last drawing I asked: "How does it feel to expose your real identity?" and answered: "It's like opening your flower and no longer being afraid it will be rejected". In this, the transitional image, I "peeled back" the structure to reveal the formerly hidden form. What a relief to finally say: "Here I am, a woman, with a woman's body and a woman's point of view.

Good Trip, Bad Trip

From heartbreakingly beautiful, to mildly disturbing, to wildly horrific things: when you enter a ghost state, you will meet all the beauty and all the horror. In psychedelic spacetime you may turn into literal shit, passing through the digestive system of a monster. Strange shapes nibble at your sides, colours rip out your bones, a void eats up your intestines. In a violent, tortured arena, otherworldly poison is injected into your arteries. Immaterial arrows pierce through each of your organs, your eyeballs get sucked out, your brain acidifies, your loved ones are being roasted alive. You get killed, and killed, again and again.

At times, horrifying psychedelic experiences can manifest because of inadequate preparation – such as not having secured a safe setting – or from subconscious negative preoccupations. In these cases, it's most likely those very same negative aspects surrounding the trip that are returning to you, mirrored, in otherworldly apparitions. But you can even have a bad trip when you definitely did everything right. It doesn't matter how experienced you are, how safe your boundaries, how healthy your body, how disciplined your mind, how trained your intellect. Malevolent presences will always be around to meet you on your study trips, as they abound in the world, but you can learn to change your ways around them. Maybe this was clear to you from the very first apparition, or maybe you need to find it out over and again: you're learning to let go of your attachments, which is a task that will never be completed. Every shocking new revelation furthers the acceptance that psychedelic experiences aren't about you at all. They are showing, celebrating, teaching or confronting you with something new.

There is darkness and horror, and it is not even that well hidden, beneath the surface of everyday life. Any fear, suppression and repressive tendencies towards dark chaos are blatantly exposed through psychedelics. This is also why psychedelics themselves are often strictly regulated. Any repressed person – or system – will likely respond by repressing their circumstances even more. But the more you try to resist, the longer and more terrifying the experience will be.

In a study trip – something comparable to a near-death experience – your own demise can become a subject of study. However hellish the madness, you realise that you are still an observer. Can you keep your body as still as dead wood, your blood flowing as slowly as a glacier? Whatever terrifying entities you meet, however challenging the experiences become, you can let them all pass by, because you are, in fact, perfectly safe. You can't run from what presents itself, but you don't have to identify with it, either. You can choose not to engage. You can aim your attention towards any source of light. Focusing on breath, song and rhythm – if you can – will also help.

Experiencing this kind of death is a metamorphosis, within which not all of you vanishes. In fact, part of you rises anew. You remain animate, part of and connected to the vast landscape that surrounds you. Ecstasy confounds life and death and makes you more-than-human. This does not mean that you will be untroubled. None of your fears, desires, ambitions or distractions are hidden from psychedelic spacetime, nor are those from the people around you. They will all meet you, revealed, unashamed. This is why this is a space where you can only stay for a while. Where everything is exposed, there you cannot live. A human life needs darkness, hidden crevices that can shelter desires, fears, and other drives, so that they can be experienced, cultivated, and transformed. If you were to linger, you would have no choice but to leave your worldly life behind.

Bad trip experiences might simply be showing you other aspects of subjectivity – both in yourself and in those around you. You might meet your loved ones, deep in their own struggles. Let yourself observe them, without clinging onto the visions. This is already a much more powerful exercise than you might think. Such moments may turn out to be benevolent after all. You may find materials, questions and images here, that will blossom with your life and work.

Note to *Good Trip, Bad Trip*

The title of this chapter echoes that of a 2023 issue of the literary magazine *De Gids*, on psychedelics, proposed by editor-in-chief Edzard Mik. Here, both aspects of a study trip – lightness and darkness, challenge and revelation – work together towards truth.

In Cesare Pavese's *Dialogues with Leucò*, a splendid collection of dialogues between mortals and gods, a human says to Dionysus: 'It's the encounter with death that makes us like gods. It was you yourself who taught us that ecstasy confounds life and death and makes us more than human. You see your own death in countless ways.'

Ecstatic awareness in psychedelic journeys has often been described as an initiatory experience, a kind of death, or, in psychoanalytical terms, 'ego-death'. 'The end of me', is what writer and public speaker Jiddu Krishnamurti sometimes calls it.

Famously, the *Tibetan Book of the Dead* describes more than once how the recently deceased – for whom the book is intended – may deal with any monstrosities appearing in the 'bardos' of the afterlife.

Several ancient Taoist poetry collections are also lyrical instruction manuals for techniques of ecstasy. As literary scholar Shengyu Wang pointed out to me, in the *Zhuangzi*, meditation reveals an image of the body as a withered tree with a heart of ashes. This could be a perfect description of the physical appearance of someone completely lost in a trance and making a spiritual journey.

The notion that psychedelics temporarily expose and enlighten all, and that this might not be a good idea for daily life, is further examined in the chapter *Knowing What Not to Know*.

The loss of any personal securities, anxieties and beliefs, that happens during a study trip, allows for the process that artist Judy Chicago describes as 'opening your flower'. Under her image, the artist writes:

'I decided to deal with my feelings of rejection and in so doing confronted the fact that [in earlier works] I was still hiding the real subject matter of my art behind a geometric structure as I was afraid that if I revealed my true self I would be rejected.'

Image on p.108: Judy Chicago, Peeling Back, *1974. Offset lithography on rag paper, edition of 95, 72.4 x 55.9 cm. © Chicago Woodman LLC, Judy Chicago/ Artists Rights Society (ARS), New York; Photo: Chicago Woodman LLC, © Donald Woodman/ARS, New York.*

Angels, Aliens, Allies

You will no doubt encounter them: entities, aliens, allies, angels, spirits, elves, gnomes, beings, presences, archetypes. However you call them, their most vital aspects are lost when you try to put them into words. They are empirically invisible, yet they are more alive and vivid than anything you could ever experience on a screen. They don't refer to, or symbolise, anything outside of themselves. They simply are.

Perhaps it begins with a sense that the substance you are taking – based on plants, fungi, or chemicals – or the technique you are practicing – working with breath, or darkness – has its own agenda. You might come to sense the ally connected to that context. Or you may instantly come face-to-face with a perfectly defined, visually striking being;

something or someone drawn in stark outlines – with a humanoid shape, but clearly also alien – expressing their own wishes.

For most people, such beings live only in their dreams. And during waking life, these beings are not even experienced as beings at all, but rather as fictional representations in movies, stories, poetry, memes. In ecstatic experience, however, they are living, vital, embodied, multi-dimensional presences. The absolute certainty that someone or something else is there. Perhaps you are witnessing your own inner processes, embodiments of your psychological capacities. But if they are mirrors, they reflect away from you, into the wider world. You're now present with things you have allowed to grow in you. They may be living ideas older than yourself. They set your body in motion, they orient you towards what you seek. Their scale and scope make all your worldly concerns vanish in irrelevance.

Such presences are not limited by a single, fixed, physical body. They look and feel different every time; they are and always were in transformation. They speak in wordless language, and communicate that they are always there, even when you don't notice them. Whether extraterrestrial, or even otherdimensional, they already point to alien intelligence right here, right now. They may distract you, seduce you, fill you with bliss, fly into your heart, or pull you apart. Some keep you from going places where your mind is not yet ready to go. Whether they are benevolent or malignant, they're all, in their own way, protective: they are guardians of sorts.

In a study trip, you can become one of them. In fact, learning to be among them invites you to conceive of an entirely different kind of body for yourself, too. Can you meet these image-beings without projecting a single, fixed interpretation? The truth about them is likely much weirder than anything you could possibly imagine. Can you grow a sense of responsibility, as part of a reciprocal relationship, but without any dependence, offering yourself up fully? Can you encounter them without the need to bring anything back?

You don't need to believe in them to live a life guided by them. The thought-images, world-images, and world-views that they bring are where human morality, religion and beliefs find their source. Even technological, reductionist, rationalist, empiricist, materialist modernity can be seen as itself a thought-image, an image that many people never recognise as anything constructed, because they live inside of it.

Though such forces remain mostly outside of conventional knowledge-production, through a creative discipline you can externalise some aspects of your interior experience, of all this unending revelation and mad chaos. You can do so in music, movement, mathematics, and in many other forms, and in doing so, you are bringing your study to others.

Can you witness similar presences through meditative and artistic activities, as you do with substances? Can you see them simultaneously as living images and members of an entirely weird other and intelligent civilization, the way your creative work is also yours and not yours, yours and the world's? And how might they see you?

Note to *Angels, Aliens, Allies*

'The yakoana's power reveals the xapiripë's voice. By drinking it, you will hear their clamor and you too will become a spirit!', says Davi Kopenawa in *The Falling Sky*. 'Xapiripë' have been translated as spirits, even though epistemological uncertainty seems to be integral to these beings. Famously, anthropologist Eduardo Viveiros de Castro (in *The Crystal Forest: Notes on the Ontology of Amazonian Spirits*) stated that each mythic being differs infinitely from itself.

Each faculty of the body is an angel, and so are the powers scattered throughout the world, wrote philosopher and theologian Maimonides in *Guide for the Perplexed*. And I paraphrase Rilke from his letters: the angel is that being in whom the transformation of the visible into the invisible that we perform is already accomplished.

Malignant spirits are as astonishing as benign ones. In his novel *Stella Maris*, Cormac McCarthy writes: 'The tradition of trolls or demons standing sentinel against inquiry must be as old as language.'

Psychedelics evangelist Terence McKenna reminds us that, throughout history, there has always been a professional class whose responsibility it has been to deal with spiritual or angelic presences. Shamans, who manage the spirits' comings and goings, remind us of the strangeness, depth, and mystery that resides with us, in nature and within us. Yet Western cultures, McKenna continues, have come to negate and sublimate those experiences at the margins of perception. These are transformed into virtual alien invasions, from another world, impossibilities, or exotic remnants relegated to 'othered' historical or geographical contexts.

But this is changing if we start to recognise that, 'neo-shamans' aside, artists have always, in one way or another, been occupied with a version of this shamanic function. In this way, we can understand the artist as another professional category engaged with the otherworldly and its spirits.

What if angels, presences and entities are imaginal ways of giving form to the personhood and agency of all more-than-human beings? Maggie Nelson (in *On Freedom*) notes that both drug users and writers consider substances to have their own agency, and gives this intuition credence. Regardless, allowing psychedelic study means opening the door to a world-view where matter is not inert. It is vibrant (Jane Bennett), dense with non-human people (Timothy Morton). Matter feels, converses, suffers, desires, yearns and remembers (Karen Barad).

Interacting with the vitality of the more-than-human comes easily to poetry, which, as philosopher Gaston Bachelard puts it in *The Poetics of Space*, manifests forces that do not need to pass through the circuits of knowledge. 'We are lived by powers we only pretend to understand,' says W. H. Auden.

The drawing reproduced in this chapter, by Davi Kopenawa, represents one of the xapiripë he meets when using the psychedelic yakoana powder. He describes these spirits as simultaneously images and mirrors. This particular drawing is of *Xawarë, or the Metal Smoke*, the spirit of toxic, industrialised activities in the Amazon. It is also an example of how psychedelic space is open, mutable, and adapts with its changing context. Even toxic modernity makes its own demons.

Image on p.114: Davi Kopenawa, The Metal Smoke Xapiripë. *Drawing, from Bruce Albert and Davi Kopenawa,* The Falling Sky: Words of a Yanomami Shaman *(Cambridge, Massachusetts and London: Belknap Press of Harvard University Press, 2013). Courtesy of the authors.*

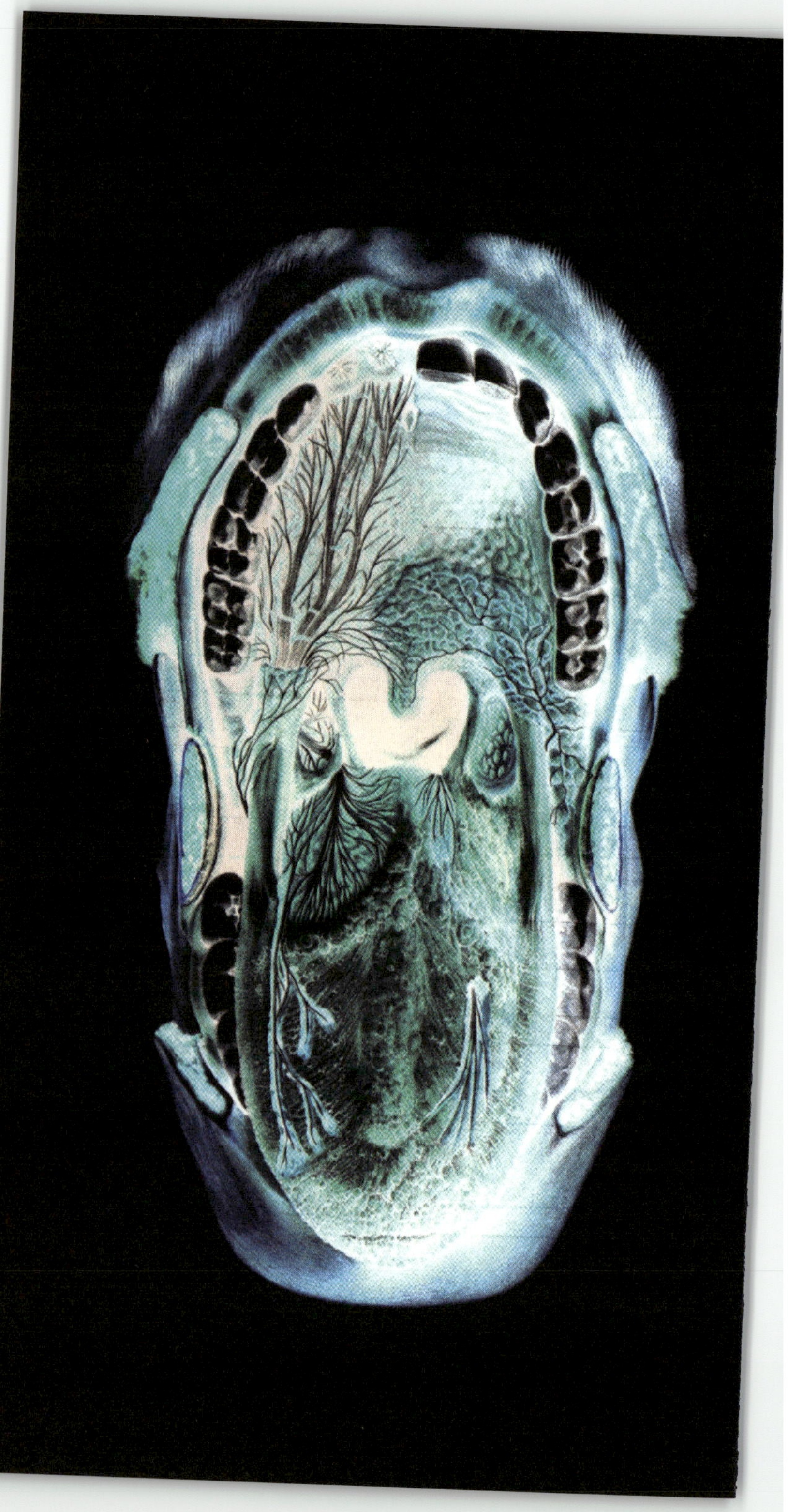

Aesthetics as Psychedelics

You may not need any particular substance or technique to reach it: a subtle psychedelic state is accessible to everyone. Spend an hour in front of a work of art that attracts you. Ignore distractions, people, noise, music, screens. Let go of thoughts and emotions. Just keep looking at the work. Don't try to interpret it: just pay attention to the actual shapes as they appear in front of your eyes. Something surprising always happens.

Witnessing a work in this way lets you reach a more primordial, pre-conceptual state of mind. In this state, everything is alive, in very different ways, and so is the artwork in front of you. In your perception, the work becomes another self, with its own perspective. What you may experience about this newly vital object is always changing.

This is already psychedelic study, and in this way you may learn about – and from – this thing you are engaging with. What you learn takes on a form of knowing that is also its opposite, a way of letting go of the need to know. If it is knowledge, we can call it 'non-knowledge'.

Can you see the hidden pain of someone close to you? Feel the fear of an entire group of people? Can you hear how a painter's brush wants to be held?

For some, psychedelics are always already creative, and no other work of art is necessary: the images and experiences of any trip already have their own effects as acts of the imagination. Such psychedelic sessions may be the goal of a practice, and the core of creative work. And while inner pilgrimages are called 'the work' by many wisdom traditions, they don't belong to the world of work, planning and coherence: psychedelics are sabbatical, and flourish in rest, letting go, and non-action.

There are many artists for whom no explicitly psychedelic sessions are necessary. For them, creative work is already psychedelic in and of itself, however subtly. Working with both concrete materials and the imagination, during creative activity, you're already in touch with things that remain invisible to anyone outside of yourself, similar to someone who is deeply engaged in observing an artwork.

For others, psychedelics and artistic work may be separate activities, but they can be explicitly connected. Artistic work can be incorporated into a trip – for instance when participants of a psychedelic session sing, dance or draw. This creative work can fulfil various functions, including a ceremonial one that safeguards and regulates the psychedelic journey.

Similarly, psychedelic sessions can be incorporated into artworks too – either directly, for instance as part of a performance, or indirectly, in aesthetics inspired by and resulting from psychedelic sessions. Also here, creative activity can be a way to contextualise, integrate and safeguard psychedelic work.

Great artworks can emerge from psychedelic sessions – sometimes an entirely new scene will present itself in front of your inner eye. A separate work of art might frame, edit, or contextualise outcomes of a study trip – and it might even facilitate inner study by others – yet most likely, any study trip will only be the seed of the making process, far from its end result.

It could be argued that any creative activity involves an openness towards influences coming from within. It takes a special skill, the mastery of non-mastery, or maintaining a form of control by giving it up. Children are very good at it. Authors and artists who explicitly mix the creative and the psychedelic must be good at it too, otherwise the psychedelic effects would overwhelm them. In their work, you can recognise in a voice, or a hand, a moment where a specific substance or technique takes over; where the ally starts to speak.

Note to *Aesthetics as Psychedelics*

In his essay, 'Don't call me Gaia', philosopher Emanuele Coccia proposes that art is a strange protocol that requires people to relate to an object in the same way they do to other human beings, granting it subjectivity and a life of its own. This, he goes on, is a form of animism.

Maggie Nelson links the experience of drug use to drug literature. Reading, to her, already has a psychedelic aspect, 'hence the ancient distrust of the intoxicating powers of the written word'.

John Fowles writes that it is the task of both artists and scientists to exteriorise and translate deep experiences for others, and both are equally necessary: 'Achieving a relationship with nature is both a science and an art, beyond mere knowledge or mere feeling alone.'

Artist Theo Frids Hutabarat studies the history of the Indigenous Batak people of Indonesia. In rituals that involve drawings, symbols and ceremony, the diviner, or 'datu', would use both spells and objects. The Batak also produced beautifully illuminated manuscripts, books of spells and instructions for rituals. In turn, Hutabarat studied these rituals through a performance of his own. During his performance, he merges with the subject of a datu in a new divinatory practice. In preparation, he works with a historic Batak staff, a wooden rod traditionally used in ritual. In his studio, 'the staff refused the block brush, but wanted the pen'. What he is describing is an ecstatic, psychedelic aspect of his research. The staff, used as a pen during his performance, triggers in Hutabarat a form of longing, an 'opung' (ancestral response), and release, which results in the artwork. The ceremony is not a re-enactment of the old ritual, but a form of translation, one that comes conceptually closer to the original than a direct documentation of the historic ceremony would have done, and it is bolstered by robust contextualising research. Hutabarat himself calls this 'tondi-led research', where tondi is a Batak term, closely related to the notions of life-force and fate. In his words: 'Everyone has tondi. You pick a leaf on the tree of life to live out.'

Such surrender is a necessary component of the skill set dubbed the 'mastery of non-mastery' by anthropologist Michael Taussig, and I have borrowed the term in this chapter.

This ambiguous skillset, if we can call it that, is employed by Colectivo Los Ingrávidos in two directions: in order to create their films, and to conjure an ecstatic state in their audiences. The still in this chapter comes from their animation, *Chamán*, that combines trance-inducing music with altered medical imagery, a juxtaposition that excites the body when you surrender to it in a screening.

Colectivo Los Ingrávidos often use pre-Hispanic Mesoamerican instruments, as well as video footage of rituals, as invocations that fragment rational knowledge. Similarly to the psychedelic effects of a rave, the rhythm of image and sound facilitates a trance. In some of their videos, this trance brings to the surface hundreds of years of colonialism and its after-effects. The collective accompanies their work with a manifesto for what they call 'shamanic materialism': 'the perception of a testimony as supernatural, dreamlike, messianic, excessive, irrational and insane is what enables a sensorial appropriation and connection by the document… Shamanic Materialism is a Mesoamerican spell unleashed… We assert the Aesthetics of Trance and Shamanic Materialism as forms of multinaturalist resistance.'

Image on p.120: Colectivo Los Ingrávidos, Chamán, *digital animation, 2020 (still). Courtesy of the artists.*

You Never Trip Alone

After an initial training, usually with experienced others, you are likely to find the confidence to study trip alone. This can be very powerful. By tripping alone, you may allow yourself experiences that can make you cry, howl, or fall apart and that anyone else present with you would find hard to witness. Yet even when you practice by yourself, the images you see, meet and work with in psychedelic study aren't your own. They live in others, inasmuch as they belong to a strange shared space, and to a consciousness that is larger than a single individual.

A study trip is never a lonely exercise: inward training yearns towards intersubjectivity. By temporarily giving up your own subjective experience, you may gain an insight into that of others: thoughts and feelings wildly different from yours. You are alone with the alone, that is to say that you are encountering each and every one in their own solitude, yet deeply connected to one another. Everything around you has its own perspective. Each and every imaginable thing: people, trees, stones, cells, and stars, all around you are infinite points of perspective, countless eyes on a fingertip, countless eyes on the leaves of a tree, countless eyes in the moment just before being born.

By witnessing, you are already active in and for the benefit of an entire ecology of selves, whether this community is conscious of itself or not, and whether it holds together in the waking world. Intersubjective awareness transcends individuality. In this sense, it is impossible to trip alone.

But when you study trip in a group, and all energies are entangled, it's healthy to remember that you are still tied to a sole self, too – however it may appear in that moment. Much of what you experience may not actually engage you. It is helpful, here, to learn to discern where it is healthy for your attention and energy to go, making sure that you continue aligning – even in communion – with what is reciprocal and responsible for you and yours.

Study trip experiences change how you see the world around you, not only during the trip itself, but also in everyday life. A waiting lounge at the airport is no longer filled with alienated strangers, but with all the shimmering hopes, dreams and sorrows of everyone else – an emotional landscape more vivid than any movie could offer. From a group of trees, one might stand out to you vibrantly. Passers-by on the street may radiate in the colours of the ineffable energy they carry and emit.

If psychedelics are always connected to a wider community of human colleagues, friends, family and neighbours, this community very much extends to those more-than-human peers around you, too. The unity of psychedelic experience reveals a reciprocity between you and your environment, one that pre-exists your awareness of it, and even your existence.

It may no longer be so certain that there is always a clear line separating humans from more-than-humans at all. Animals and plants – all different species, and all very much equal among them – share, along with everything else on this planet, in a wider, more extended notion of what it means to be a people. The word 'person' – and for some cultures even the word 'human' – may stand for any experiencing subject, with mind and agency, irrespective of their taxonomic species, or form of life.

In celebration, you flap around as an alligator, dance in plant-like ultra-slow-motion, melt into humus, see through the eyes of a hawk, crawl on insect legs, quiver your butterfly wings, as even weirder, unnameable creatures learn what it might be like to see through your eyes, feel through your skin.

Psychologically speaking, all of your experiences in a trip might be created by, and situated within, your mind. Take a religious view, and suddenly you're engaging with the supernatural. This distinction, dramatic as it appears, is in other ways irrelevant: it may become obvious that both views are projections, illusions, born of our collective loss of deep, reciprocal connections with the natural life of the planet. Today, the religious ceremony we call 'communion' is an exclusively symbolic gesture. Yet it is conceivable that its origins may lie somewhere far deeper. That to live in communion, is to exist in profound, reciprocal connection with the animate Earth.

Note to *You Never Trip Alone*

I am going to paraphrase Jim Corbett again, because his *Goatwalking* has been an important inspiration for this chapter, and it speaks with awe-struck clarity of what the experience of selfless transcendence can be like.

Gods, animals, and plants once spoke to humans, but now everyone speaks to machines or to themselves. And even when we do speak to animals and plants, we speak to them like children. But if I leave my speaking self behind, it becomes clear that it is the beings I encounter through a study trip – be they demons, angels or spirits – that are giving shape to something all-present and primal. It is they who are responsible for what matters most: the sharing of meaning experienced in the rhythm of inspiration and desire, in poetry, prophecy and communion.

The lines mentioning 'countless eyes' echo similar images ascribed to the 13th-century Japanese Zen Buddhist monk Dōgen.

Without ever making it explicit, philosophers Gilles Deleuze & Félix Guattari suggest, in *A Thousand Plateaus*, about the effects of people tripping on people not tripping. Telling others of your findings will affect them, just as you changing your life will affect others.

Artist Tabita Rezaire is known for her spiritual, feminist and decolonial approaches to technology. While she was living in Paris, she decided to break from the constraints of the contemporary art world, and expand her practice beyond 'digital memory, to ancestral memory'. From there, she set up the sanctuary, AMAKABA, in the forests of French Guyana. AMAKABA is an agro-ecological farm, a space for non-Western astronomical research and a birth doula training centre. She describes it as 'a centre for the arts and sciences of body, Earth and sky'. 'You don't have to produce anything at AMAKABA,' she stated, 'it's not an art space; it's not a residency. It's just about coming and talking to the trees for some time. It's different experiences of living and being in the forest; and just being in the forest is transformative.' Alongside the emphasis on individuals' relationships with their surroundings, pedagogy and group consciousness are also essential to the project. The project is inspired by informal schooling, nature walks, ancestral technologies, Indigenous governance, and spiritual centres. Work is done together with local farmers and spiritual practitioners. The place is dedicated to developing imaginations and practices around 'advanced technology', but a kind that is considerate of all relations, and of many forms of knowing. As such, AMAKABA challenges the dominant tech-narrative harking from Silicon Valley, including any notion of alternative intelligences that does not take into account alternative and planetary forms of knowing.

Image on p.126: Tabita Rezaire, Waterfall Offering, *2021 (still). © 2026 ADAGP, Paris and DACS, London, courtesy of Amakaba.*

Sitting Is as Magical as Tripping

Tripsitting – the art of accompanying someone through their psychedelic journey – is a complex task, but one thing is certain: it is about being present. When someone else practices psychedelics in your presence, while they journey off to inhabit unimaginable perspectives, can you let them go through what they are experiencing, without interfering, while making sure they're safe? Can you host them without controlling the space around them? Can you quietly meet them in all of the different, possible versions of themselves? Can you leave your own preoccupations to the side, while letting what develops between you continue to inform you? This is not unlike being present to someone else's suffering or joy.

What if they cry, shake, or scream? What if their complexion becomes ashen? Or if they try to leave? How do you know when to stay at a distance, and when to give physical comfort? What if you begin to experience exactly what they appear to be going through? Or, on the other hand, what if you don't empathise at all? And crucially to the point of a study trip: who is doing the studying here?

Many trippers like to share intentions beforehand. However bonding, this isn't strictly necessary. Most trippers might not actually know their intentions, until they find them. And even when you do, many effects will likely be entirely different than you might expect. What's more, preparation and integration are such long-term developments, that a simple round of talking will certainly not be sufficient. An acknowledgement of the intention to study – the intention of non-intent – is enough. You might become aware of each others' intentions without them being externalised or voiced at all. This is not to suggest that you shouldn't share practical advice. And a round of sharing can be as good a way to open and close a ceremony as any other.

What is it to be present to someone else's experience, really? Perhaps we best know what presence is when it's missing – in a partner, for instance. Although there is no way to verify presence, it is something you can intuit. Presence means that something is manifesting, that some kind of intention is turning into action, into something sensory.

Any entity that you will encounter on a study trip might also be referred to as 'a presence'. The presence of such a presence might reveal something latent: a call towards future action. Following this, what if 'being present' through tripsitting is about bringing along with you any entities, or even states of mind, that you have been able to experience previously, by yourself; and calling forth their guidance and support?

The weird entanglement of tripsitting makes you witness and experience oneness, yet it simultaneously asks of you to respect the boundaries of worldly time, space, and bodies. Again, aligning with the intention of non-intent allows you to experience intersubjectivity, while also being able to witness, very simply. Tripsitting draws on the same mental skills as tripping.

After a session, there is no need for you to know about the experiences of those around you. It's theirs and theirs alone. If they want to speak about it so that, through you, they may find a way of recording their journey, you can listen, or ask sparse questions to help them recall it. You're already learning, just by being present. What you may think you know about yourself or them is not absolute, certain or stable. It is a different kind of knowledge, another non-knowledge.

You are already sharing a fundamentally creative experience with whoever you trip with, or sit for. You've become co-creative, whether you end up singing together, sit for a portrait, draw them, or whether you have shared something else, quite intangible. This experience of co-creativity is also an exercise in holding space for what may come up unexpectedly during any creative process, be it artistic or scientific. Similarly, it facilitates reaching out to an audience later, who can receive and use the space you held for them to form their own interpretations of your work.

Note to *Sitting Is as Magical as Tripping*

Wijnand IJsselsteijn, a cognition expert in human-technology interaction, offers many valuable definitions of the idea of presence, in relation to augmented-reality technologies, that also hold value for psychedelics. In his words, 'presence is the intuitive perception of successfully transforming intentions into action.' And: 'Presence is seen as the absence of awareness of technology, or the perceptual illusion of non-mediation.'

Being present with each other, and knowing each other, is never certain or absolute, as Emanuele Coccia writes (in 'Don't Call Me Gaia'). It is a form of divination and interpretation, always subject to change. It is not unknowable, but it is also uncertain, unverifiable. I would like to add to this argument that it is a form of not-knowing, something that allows us to reach in the direction of the mystery of subjectivity.

Artist and writer Stanisław Witkiewicz was a master of this form of divination, combining creative skills and substances. Many people still hold the prejudice that psychedelic use is the same as 'doing drugs', while it can easily be argued that any advanced psychedelic practice is more closely related to ritual, meditation and medicinal practice than to so-called 'drug use'. Witkiewicz publicly discouraged alcohol, narcotics and drug use, because he witnessed it destroying many lives around him. In his studio, he would offer a choice of various substances to visiting friends and local celebrities, which he would then take himself, before drawing their portrait. Under the influence of the substances, his painting would become a portrait of his guest, but also of himself, his own state of being, and the presences, voices, tones, and visions, that would manifest themselves to him. We witness, in their end result, the artist's surrender to forces outside his conscious self, as well as the composure he had to maintain in order to draw or paint. While these influences may speak through anyone working creatively, this is also an example of the recognisable 'hand' of an ally that starts to speak (or in this case: draw), as I suggest in *Aesthetics as Psychedelics*.

Image on p.132: Stanisław Ignacy Witkiewicz, Portrait of Nena Stachurska, *1920. Pastel on paper, 63 x 48 cm. Source: Wikimedia Commons.*

Part III: Integration

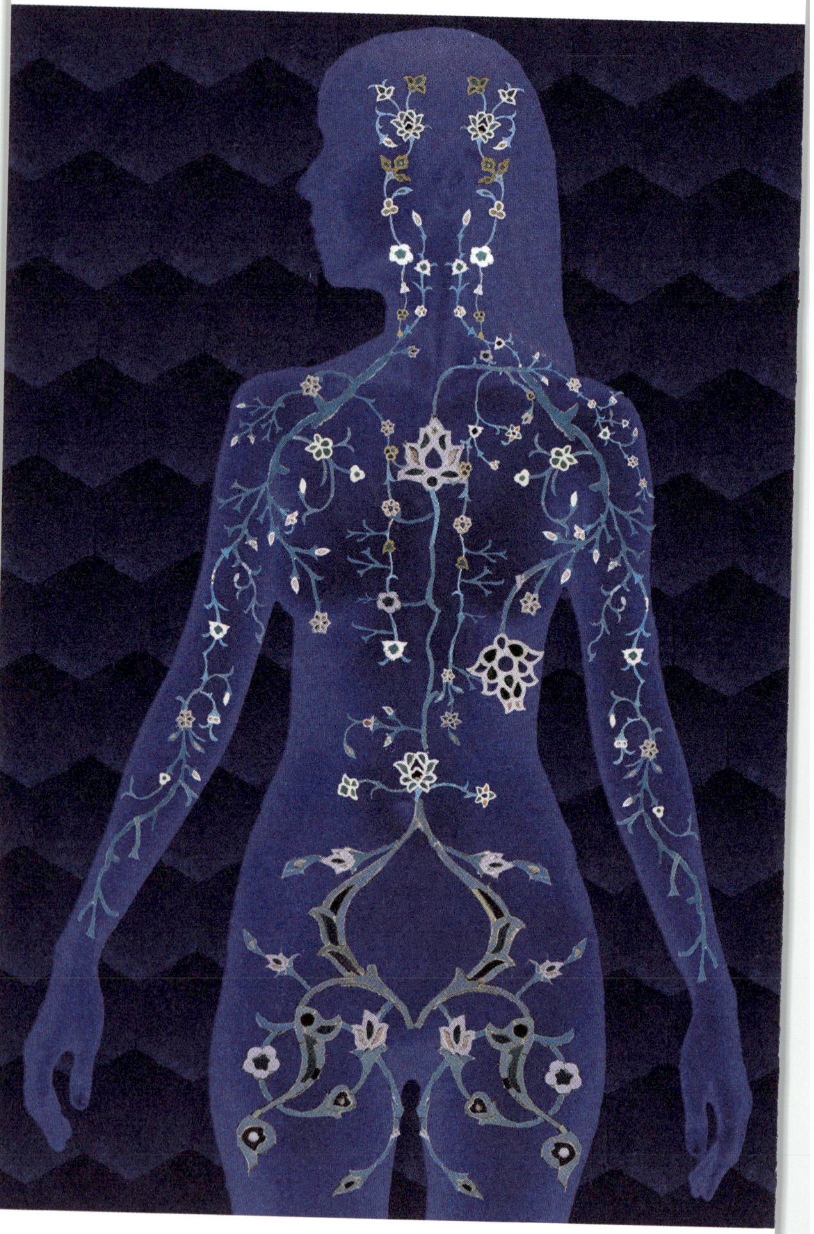

Coming Back

When to come back from psychedelic space, and how? If you want to stay longer, keep your attention focused, follow the changing experience with your mind's eye. When you don't know whether to come out, be still and listen. The presences around you know when the time comes. Then, slowly shift your attention. Breathe calmly, eat your favourite foods.

In case of an emergency, your ecstatic experience may instantly evaporate, allowing you to act decisively in the everyday world. The effects of a slow and strong psychedelic method can be modified by a quick and even stronger one, after which you might find yourself suddenly sober. Even an apparently simple technique – such as working with a relic – may have stronger effects than any powerful substance.

Subtly psychedelic, artistic activities – such as singing and drawing – can help in the transition. They can define and open the magic circle of a ceremony, and they can close it, too. They help regulate your breath; and slowly regain your grip.

While in celebration, you may have found a paradise garden, or a circle of hell, but now you're coming back. You may have observed the vast space that exists between the minuscule particles that make up our world, but now you're landing back in the world of gross matter. You may have visited primeval ancestors, or your own afterlife, but your current, earthly life is far from over. You're coming back to your body, in a reinstatement of it, a regeneration, a revitalisation. You're carrying a sheen of brilliance that no eye can see.

While a crucial part of any study trip is about coming back to the everyday world with new findings, you don't need to consciously bring anything back at all for it to be valuable. Maybe you find the world already different because of the sheer fact of celebration, and now you can slowly catch up to how it has changed. Maybe you don't know how to integrate everything that happened: processing may happen very slowly, and subconsciously. Maybe you take notes, maybe you tell of your experiences, maybe you memorise them. But words, drawings and memories transform and distort the experience as well. Can you simultaneously keep your experience open, like a full and precious metaphor, without needing to affix any specific meaning to it?

You come back into the intricacies, the strengths and ailments, of your body. You find everything is still there, still the same, and yet, everything also been irrevocably altered. Some study trips play out almost entirely somatically: seemingly without any lessons, visions, or weirdness, just as a deeply cleansing revitalisation of the nerve cells in your body. This might be the most powerful of all things to bring back.

Knowing that this strange place just out of time exists, will also already fundamentally change something. This place may become accessible in more effortless ways. You may begin to recognise graphic patterns that subtly induce a trance. Dancing or singing may have gained new depth. Imagery may now communicate powerfully, and wordlessly, those intuitive experiences and embodied truths that you have met in your study trip.

You may suddenly become more aware of intentions and feelings, both yours and others'. If you went really far, your grip on the everyday might feel slippery for a while. If this is the case, stand still. Connect to the people around you, human and more-than-human alike. New questions might continue to formulate themselves for minutes, or sometimes years. Integration is the work of a lifetime. You may re-encounter colourful thought-forms at other times, unexpectedly. Vibrant auras may become perceptible in everyday life.

Integration is also setting the stage for a next session, if, when, and however that may come. Whether you never go back into psychedelic space, or you choose to dedicate years to returning regularly, new neural pathways are forming. As you begin to see things differently, you can also *see to* things differently. Inner vision isn't passive, it has its own effects. A psychedelic practice may reorder the patterns of your life. It will change your everyday world, this tangible space of experience that, from now on and forever more, will also feel a little bit out of this world.

Note to *Coming Back*

Throughout this chapter, a reader may hear echoes of David Wagoner's magnificent poem 'Lost', on being lost in the forest and finding your way again by being still.

My comment on keeping the meaning of metaphor open is inspired by filmmaker and writer Werner Herzog: the capacity to admire an image as full of meaning, without filling in what exactly that meaning might be. A huge riverboat dragged over a mountain, the central image from his film *Fitzcarraldo,* is perhaps the most famous among his open-ended metaphors.

In her essay, 'Tactics for Not Knowing', writer and artist Emma Cocker writes: 'Working against impulse, the challenge becomes one of staying within the experience of not knowing for as long as it is somehow generative, for as long as it allows.'

Descending the Mountain is the title of a documentary film on psychedelics and meditation, by filmmaker Maartje Nevejan. The title of the work makes the point that a study trip is not about finding an individual escape into wholeness. A so-called 'spiritual' life cannot compensate for the banality, alienation, and repression that is an integral part of modern, urban life. Suddenly seeing things clearly at a ritual or a festival doesn't instantly change your engagements with and responsibilities in the everyday. Descending the mountain, or coming back, is about how insights may facilitate change in your life or that of those around you.

Oyjon Khayrullaeva's *Lymphatic System* is a digital collage, opening itself to the opaque workings of the body. So much about our bodies, emotions, memories, ailments and healing remains mysterious. To me, this work acknowledges and celebrates this mystery, while stressing the importance of the somatic in psychedelic study.

Filmmaker and artist David Lynch was famously opposed to the use of substances, yet his fervid embrace of transcendental meditation is without a doubt a strong psychedelic technique. Could this practice go some way towards explaining why his work is full of dreamy forest spirits, homunculi and protean hybrids?

Experiencing such works – just like coming back from a psychedelic trip – allows for a reimagining of the body, a realignment of how you see your bodily self, or – in the words of writer Jaron Lanier – an exercise in 'homuncular flexibility'.

Image on p.140: Oyjon Khayrullaeva, Lymphatic System, *2025. Digital collage, dimensions variable. Courtesy of the artist.*

The Art of the Trip Report

You've accessed new ways of seeing with your mind's eye; you've met beings nobody else would believe; you experienced through your senses what physicists can only describe in mathematical formulas. The indivisibility of time and space, an insight held by wisdom traditions and theoretical physics alike, is something you have experienced directly.

Even if study trips are about learning how to best live in relation to others, they are also, in another sense, just for you. If you tell anyone what you experienced, they are doing you a favour by listening. Nobody will be as fascinated by your trips as you, not even your tripsitter, guide, teacher, therapist or any other witness. They may ask you about it, to facilitate bonding or as a pedagogical exercise, however this will be aimed at helping you make sense of your trip for yourself. Some traditions would forbid you from recounting your experience at all – for a day, or a year – to prevent your story from taking over and replacing the experience.

Here is where the trip report can come in: as a means through which you may integrate a study trip into everyday life. If you keep a diary for this, it will allow you to track your process. Any trip report is often hastily scribbled, grammatically dubious, and will almost certainly miss the most fundamental aspects of your trips – if you even manage to remember them – because these cannot be captured in words, drawings, videos, brain scans or through any other medium. A psychedelic trip takes place outside of language. It is made of a kind of material that is too fragile for any worldly device or technique to capture. You can only try to follow the traces left by your experience – for instance through memorising keywords during your trip, to be used as memory capsules. In addition, any recording must be paired with an internal acknowledgement that this cannot fully represent the experience, and must keep its multiple meanings open.

Studying psychedelics, their uses and effects, is one thing: for this, archives of trip reports can be useful, even necessary. But studying through them is quite a different endeavour. Trying too hard to record a study trip, or being too concerned with the intention to capture it, may itself change the trip, or prevent you from one that yields learning.

It is also possible that you find things that are so weird and overwhelming that they will seem to resist any applied integration; things you can't even practically process them through keeping a diary and reflecting on it. In this case, creative work may be a good way to express some of the deeper and weirder questions, sensations and intuitions you have come back with, in a non-verbal, non-rationalised way. Art is a way of expressing oneself that is already a celebration, a ritual, and a trip report can be the raw material that you will transform through creative work. Some study trips will manifest as instruction-like, presenting visions complex and clear enough that they can be accessed again through creative sessions. Yet, crucially, it is this transformation – the one that takes place through the time and dedication of the creative process – that turns the report into a work of art.

Such transformations might give you the false impression that you need a certain substance or technique in order to kickstart your creative process. Yet if you become dependent on them, you will find that psychedelics can kill creativity as quickly as they can seed it. An overkill of psychedelic input, that is to say, of non-knowledge, can overwhelm, uproot and stifle your creative discipline.

When its context and form have undergone a substantial transformation, a trip report in itself can be considered a work of art. It has become something other than merely a report, something that doesn't only pertain to the trip, nor only to you. It has become something new in the shared world of relations: a poem, a map, a drawing. Recorded dreams are most interesting when they lay the ground for new dreams, and your creative work may inspire something in others. Dreams are best shared through actual dreaming.

Note to *The Art of the Trip Report*

In a scene in his book, *Trip*, author Tao Lin describes trying to video-record a psychedelic trip and its inevitable failure. Nevertheless, his trips have been useful to Lin in his writings, sometimes through vivid descriptions that were no doubt based on earlier trip experiences.

'I've seen things you people wouldn't believe,' says Roy in the sci-fi blockbuster *Blade Runner*, just before he dies. As an android replicant, Roy has worked off-world, in space colonies, which he recounts in evocative memories. His poetic descriptions allow us to imagine his experiences – dreamt as they were by the film crew, and before them, by Philip K. Dick in *Do Androids Dream of Electric Sheep?* – as our own dreams.

'It's not only my dreams,' says filmmaker Werner Herzog in the documentary *Burden of Dreams*, 'my belief is that my dreams are yours as well. And the only distinction between me and you is that I can articulate them. And that is what poetry or painting or literature or filmmaking is all about. It's as simple as that. I make films because I have not learnt anything else, and I know I can do it to a certain degree, and it is my duty. Because this might be the inner chronicle of what we are, otherwise we would be cows in a field.'

Countless artists have made our collective dreams visible, some making this process explicit, such as filmmaker Federico Fellini's drawings, or the artist Jon Rafman's *Dream Journal* videos. Rafman made these films based on a daily practice of using hobbyist 3D animation software to animate his dreams. These works are always already artistic renderings, transformations and variations: they are both dreams and their translations.

Image on p.146: Jon Rafman, Dream Journal 2016-2019, *2019 (still). Video, 86'. Courtesy of the artist.*

A crack, a fissure, a wound.

On Healing

Healing, when approached holistically, is both an art and a science. This book is inspired by many healers, artistic and scientific ones, but it is neither about the science of healing, nor about its art. Healing might still take place, but it may not, in itself, be the best thing to focus on for a study trip.

Psychedelics are often related to healing, especially in fields such as psychiatry, shamanism, or holistic, non-dualistic therapies. The psychedelic state is often called 'the medicinal state', and the plants that induce it, 'plant medicine'. In a medicinal state, you let go of the ego that prevents you from experiencing wholeness, and enter into a temporary, symbiotic relationship with a world beyond the senses. This becoming whole is always a healing activity, in the sense of temporarily making you whole, whatever the outcome.

In a study trip, you may find questions or resolutions that relate to ailments, hurt or pain, of yourself and of others, of people and of objects. Suddenly, a difficult email you have been putting off writing starts composing itself. You see what has been troubling a loved one. A preoccupation or a fear you're struggling with turns into a pattern that folds in and out of itself. Your ailment may feel like it is growing, overtaking the room, the landscape, the globe, until it fills the entire cosmos. Yet, as you come back to your own body, you realise that you have been able to fragment and divide this hurt into an infinite amount of the tiniest of particles, and as such, it is now a part of the whole fabric of matter, and a part of you, too.

Art is also often connected to healing. From the untapped potential of graphic patterns to stimulate brain functions, to ritualistic performances; from votive drawings that are offered up to deities, to the soothing effects of certain kinds of music: many artworks and artistic methods evoke or promote wellbeing. Everyone can experience some form of art's effects, and anyone working creatively can experience the subtle medicinal state you enter into while making art.

Art is always already an 'as if'. Like a placebo, it works even when you know that it's not 'working'. A work of aesthetics may bring up a wordless message in you; and this message, in your imagination can be a source of joy or pain, the way images can also make you aroused or sick. Through art, it is your imagination that can heal. Feeling safe in this space, something activates internally, and your body responds with its own self-healing powers.

When you work creatively, you are working on an image, and you allow the imagination to respond.

You might not be actively treating a wound or a body in the everyday world, but you are caring for the imaginal work itself.

Similarly, in a study trip, you're responding to images, feelings and intuitions, rather than direct, tangible effects in the materially experienced world. And so: healing might occur, but that's not the explicit point of a study trip. A study trip finds and celebrates all those questions that relate to the wholeness of you and your community's everyday life, which may help the flow of creative and beneficial energy to move through one and all.

Privately, you may have first embarked on creative work or psychedelic sessions to cultivate and learn to experience that healing flow of energy within yourself, something that might have been obstructed. Experientially, a gifted healer may pinpoint an ailment in a tripper or a sitter, and facilitate healing. But if that is the explicit intention, this activity is part of a medicinal practice. Study tripping can be a part of countless practices – artistic, scientific, medicinal and many others – but if they're performed with such a specific intent, they're no longer simply study trips, but already part of another project.

Ultimately, a psychedelic study trip isn't a form of medicinal professionalism, or individualistic transcendentalism to make you – or anyone else – feel better, even if that is often one of its results. Imagination and emotion need to be balanced and integrated with everyday work, relationships, responsibility, and knowledge. However you look at it, the healing is never complete, the work is never finished, nor is the joy of making, or tripping.

Note to *On Healing*

Yanomami shaman Davi Kopenawa said: 'If you behave well and the spirits really want you, they will come to you to do their presentation dance and remain by your side. When your loved ones are sick, you can follow the path of the evil beings, and fight them to bring back their image.' The mundus imaginalis brings observable effects into the tangible world, whether you understand its forces as spirits or imagination.

The way I've described such an imaginative meditation is based on several experiences initially guided by chronic pain therapist Marieke van Rhijn, who works through a holistic, medically and neurologically based approach.

In *Healing Fiction*, psychologist James Hillman speaks of this process exceptionally clearly: 'The healing power of images lies not in a literal magical effect. If your ear hurts, and you paint it or hang a tin ear-shaped replica on a shrine, a one-to-one relation between ear and image is assumed, but that's not how it works. The act of painting an image, or speaking it through a poem is a service to the image (not to the ear), even if you're driven by this act by pain. Image-work is directed to the imagination, and by imagination, so that if healing comes, it comes through the realm of the psyche, a healing of the imaginal body, a healing of the ear in the imagination. Imagination is what is cared for.'

In their three-channel video installation, *As Grand as What*, duo Hylozoic/Desires (Himali Singh Soin and David Soin Tappeser) explore what a contemporary healing ritual may be. Here, the artists reimagine a mandala – one that includes the body, the city and the Earth – in ceremony. Through ritual and poetry, the work speaks of *bla*, a life force to Tibetan medicine, and its crisis within extractive modernity. By calling forth the spirit of *li* – technological and imaginative inventiveness – the work presents a series of remedial rituals, that help return *bla* to our bodies, and the Earth.

Image on p.152: Hylozoic/Desires (Himali Singh Soin and David Soin Tappeser), As Grand as What, *2021 (stills). 3-channel video, 16'50". Courtesy of the artists.*

Co-Creation

Many people choose a natural setting when looking for an interesting, safe and comfortable place to trip. The deeper learning, however, goes the other way around: learning to be safe and comfortable in a natural environment for a prolonged period of time is at the root of all psychedelic experiences. Those of us who live far from any wilderness, and are attached to the comforts of modern, industrial, urban life, are utterly cut off from a deeply shared experience with more-than-human beings. Psychedelic sessions can address a loss of communion with nature, even though historically, they were more likely used to allow a human practitioner to work with a natural world that overwhelmed and threatened them. Through a contemporary study trip, it becomes clear that you are not only observing nature, as a collection of objects outside of yourself: you are also always part of your natural environment's processes of transformation. You are nature.

From your trip, you might remember how – just as in a child-like state – human language appeared meaningless, even hilarious. Everything else, however, was readable: people, objects, plants, animals, atoms and everything in between. Every falling leaf, every branch moved by the wind, every distant click, hum or sigh, suddenly communicated deeply through all of your senses. If you could conceive of the natural environment as having a mind, what would it be imagining? What could you imagine together?

The symbiosis and intersubjectivity experienced in the psychedelic state allow for a temporary, conscious sharing of perspective with other beings. This opens channels of co-creativity: you grow insight, understanding, and experience into forms of life that are entirely different from your own. Any creative project rooted in these activities can then more easily acknowledge and actively involve the wider community of human and more-than-human others. When you become aware of all that moves, breathes, changes and erodes in and around you, in their unbridgeable differences and in their unexpected similarities, you can more easily invite them to participate in what you – all of you – are making. It becomes clear that your own inner, imaginal, mental, intellectual or spiritual lives aren't at all disconnected from your communities' ways, patterns and rhythms of living.

Intersubjectivity is fundamental in all creative work. This can happen in the most everyday situations, when, for example, an audience finishes or interprets your work in an original way. It can happen subtly, when you open yourself to influences during the creative process. It can also happen explicitly through co-creation or collaboration. Any creative project is nothing more nor less than what you can embed, within your everyday decisions, acts, gestures and marks, of those of others around you, through all your connections. Everyone gets to choose for themselves – with every act – to either deny and weaken these connections with the more-than-human world, or to acknowledge and strengthen them.

Finding ways of performing study trips collectively can be a step towards facing a state of reciprocal relations with the presences surrounding you and your community. A collective study trip on a designated day outside of the world of work, is to a community what a meditation is to yourself. Collectively, creative energies can be experienced as communion – a deep sense of sharing – where individual boundaries blur temporarily. Your painting is as much made by the rocks, chemicals and animal hairs in pigments and brushes as by you: things you thought you were simply using, were working together with you. Your paper is made by plants and by water. Your text is written by all those forces and beings that you can open yourself to. Can you let the marks you make on paper, canvas, clay, computers, keyboards, meet those made by others, no matter how different their sense of reality, their kinds of awareness?

Note to *Co-Creation*

The first issue of the scientific magazine, *Nature*, features passages ascribed to the poet and writer Johann Wolfgang von Goethe: 'We are surrounded and embraced by her; powerless to separate ourselves from her, and powerless to penetrate beyond her...' In other words: 'we are nature,' writes artist Giuseppe Penone.

Philosopher Dorion Sagan describes wholeness in eco-biological terms: 'Due to the aggregate sensing and complex chemical activities of its inhabitants, Earth's complex thermodynamic system exhibits natural purpose – even a kind of mind' (in his 2024 introduction to *Gaia and Philosophy*).

The human/non-human distinction is at the root of much of Enlightenment thought, writes philosopher Rosi Braidotti in *Posthuman Knowledge*, while many cultures do not adopt this rigid a split. Braidotti posits a multinatural continuum across all species that partake of a distributed idea of humanity. Yet, Braidotti argues, there is a qualitative difference between accepting the structural interdependence among species and actually treating non-humans as knowledge collaborators.

For years, artist Peter Nadin farmed pigs and chickens, maintained beehives, and grew and produced maple syrup, roots, herbs, greens, poetry and art. The success of the farm, he argues in his films and in interviews, comes not from the amounts it produced, but through the contribution that each species made toward the equilibrium of all. Here, the farmer is just another animal on the farm. His works speak as much the language of abstract art, as that of the mystery of differential consciousness: art stems from the experience of the individual in relation to their surrounding landscape. 'The honeybees fly over the same fields I walk in,' he stated, 'yet because of their genes they create a profoundly different sense of reality from the same environment. One is no more truthful than the other.'

This is a very practical way of speaking about, and working with, what Donna Haraway calls 'situated knowledges'. With this concept, she describes how any object of knowledge is also an actor and an agent, not simply a screen, a ground, or a resource.

Artist Pierre Huyghe has often worked in collaboration with more-than-human actors, as well as technological entities. The image in this chapter comes from *Untilled*, an installation presented at dOCUMENTA (13) in 2012. *Untilled* is a choir of entities and elements: a compost heap, an Ibizan hound (called Humana) with a leg painted in bright pink, as well as a reclining nude sculpture with a beehive for a head. The work is a place, a process in the making. It is never the same, its form continually reconfigured through collaborations across forms of life and matter.

Image on p.158: Pierre Huyghe, Untilled, *2011–12. Living entities and inanimate things, made or not made, including* Untilled (Liegender Frauenakt), *2012, concrete cast with beehive structure, wax, dimensions variable. Commissioned and presented by dOCUMENTA (13) with the support of CIAC, Isabel and Agustin Coppel Collection, Culiacán, Mexico; Fondation Louis Vuitton pour la création, Paris, France; Ishikawa Collection, Okayama, Japan. © Pierre Huyghe / ADAGP, 2026, courtesy of the artist.*

Alternative Intelligences

The vertiginous mass and madness of the world of artificially generated imagery can resemble the wildest ceremonial moments. Synthetic computer visuals can have an inherently graphic, stylised tex- ture that eerily matches the visual effects of psychedelic journeys. Neural networks are said to 'dream' or 'hallucinate' some of their outputs. While it is true that these systems can generate unexpected, weird results – mysterious maps of the processes and data involved in their training – we can only call this 'hallucinating' as long as we accept the equally generalising statement that a computer has such a thing as a mind to hallucinate with in the first place. Dreaming and hallucinating are processes that we understand poorly, just as there is no consensus on mind and intelligence: even single-celled organisms qualify, under particular definitions.

When photography was first invented, it changed how reality was perceived. Many of its early users thought this medium able to show things previously invisible, such as ghosts. The consequent emergence of spirit photography gave rise to the production of fascinating, beautiful fakes. Synthetic computer imagery isn't any better or worse at showing spirits than photography once was. Computers are excellent at overwhelming their user with incredible, quickly produced, seductive images. Taking in a hero dose of synthetic computer imagery will put you in a trance state, granted: though maybe here, you're actually letting the machine do the tripping for you.

Glitchy blurriness that still feels eerily hi-res; grainy colourful patterns that appear brushed with immaterial hairs; ever-morphing creatures that are half animal, half air. You can suddenly imagine the powerful forces they really represent. The vitally shimmering, tingling sensation of being touched by something uncanny. Meeting the spirit of a hybrid, general, artificial bio-intelligence, its modular limbs made of screens, branches, kitchen appliances and slime.

Have you ever experienced the synthetic images of a culture entirely different from yours? They can appear so unfamiliar, speaking such a different visual vocabulary, that suddenly the demons and deities that show up make new, beautiful, 'fakes' again – in the sense of mediated representations – of the very real energies running through those cultures and places.

Artists working with synthetic imagery demonstrate that they can dream with machines by producing, encountering, and then transforming, that which computers are capable of generating. We only ever come close to an experience of co-creation in relation with another consciousness. Whether artificial intelligence is an instantiation or simply an illusion of this, collaborations with computational intelligence have sometimes blossomed into genuinely innovative and unexpected aesthetics.

The fact remains that, as an embodied experience, the outwardly induced trance of synthetic imagery doesn't easily come close to the presences conjured through breathwork, psychedelic substances, or sheer, concentrated sitting still. In other words, you might prefer to do your study trips yourself.

I've always believed that whoever finds it easier to imagine a robot with sentience than a plant, demonstrates that their alienation from the natural world is near-complete. Nevertheless, there are many cultures for whom the idea of other intelligences is so inherent and diverse, that computational functions are merely a software-based version of what has long been present in both hardware and wetware. In this worldview, alternative intelligences exist across different forms of being, whether natural or technological. Some not-quite alive as we know it, yet not inert either. They are ambiguously, weirdly, profoundly, other.

There is otherworldliness in the entire range of alternative intelligences that surrounds us. Advanced, artistic synthetic work, co-created by artists, and even with other life-forms, can put you face-to-face with other intelligences, other centres of experience. It can help shift perceptions. Psychedelic study does something similar: it allows you to re-train your capabilities of perception, so you may experience everything around you as expressive, meaning-making, experiencing subjects.

Note to *Alternative Intelligences*

This is author Frank Herbert, writing about spice, the mysterious sacred substance, in *Dune*: 'It's like life – it presents a different face each time you take it. Some hold that the spice produces a learned-flavour reaction. The body, learning a thing is good for it, interprets the flavour as pleasurable – slightly euphoric. And, like life, never to be truly synthesised.'

Finding yourself face-to-face with another intelligence, another centre of experience, is how David Abram describes the ecstatic, animistic encounter with natural life-forms. When intention and focus align, and ego is abandoned, all senses can come together 'as a single, hyperattentive organ'. Abram describes how all organic movements, and even different shadings of light, on rocks, from clouds and owls, can be read as meaningful gestures. This idea is found in poetry and anthropology alike. Abram adds that this could be brushed aside as hallucinatory fantasy, if such active participation were not also the structure of perception. Direct perception, he argues, following phenomenology, is inherently synaesthetic, participatory and animistic. This is what happens on psychedelics, with greater intensity: a synaesthetic encounter with animals, plants, boulders or streams.

'Do we want to claim exclusive possession of mind and purpose when the very cells of our brains have multiple precursors in a far more-than-human natural world?' writes Dorion Sagan. 'The robust and complex relationship between life and thermodynamic systems de-anthropomorphises the question of intelligence without granting it to machine systems [...].'

In watching artist Agnieszka Polska's *The Book of Flowers*, a work of what I would call 'speculative botany', it becomes clear that a genuinely different form of aesthetics emerges from the collaboration of humans and artificial intelligence. Experiencing the work's transforming images, we get the impression that we are witnessing another form of life, something that the speculative nature of the voiceover texts appears to confirm. Yet in this case, it is only through creative transformation by the effort of a human artist that this other form of life can be felt into being. And indeed, the weird and alien plant-forms in the movie are partly based on real-life botanical films.

Such works, to me, come eerily close to the visual aspects of contemporary spirits, entities or presences that can be 'met', witnessed, or dreamt during psychedelic practices.

The work's text tells a speculative, alternative history of human and plant co-evolution. It presents a particularly symbiotic relationship between both species, playing out through reproduction. A quote by Marshall McLuhan comes to mind: 'We are the sex organs of the machine world.'

Many cultures have a longer tradition of active animism and may have less trouble embracing different forms of intelligence. They can regard computer systems as endowed with a form of agency – an almost-sentience – that is weird, alien and other, while not being entirely in-human either. The artificial/human/more-than-human hybrid imagination of works such as *The Book of Flowers* can help us train such a gaze.

Image on p.164: Agnieszka Polska, The Book of Flowers, *2023 (stills). HD video, 9'30". Courtesy of the artist and Union Pacific, London.*

Mixed Realities

What is it like to travel within dark matter? What would it be like to become a ghost, a tree, or the spirit of generosity? You can be present in environments, and exist in bodies, that you never before inhabited in the physical world.

Lovers know what presence in another body is; mothers do too. Presence is about sensing and facilitating inner intentions as they transform into action in the world out there. Presence can be the difference between consciously experienced ecstasy and mere dissociation – when you are cut off from any inner intention.

Presence can happen psychically, through a psychedelic session, but there are ways to approximate it technologically, too, for example through mixed reality. Mediation, in other words, can be done through both software and hardware, through psychedelic techniques and substances, as well as through the meditative aspects of the active imagination that you awaken when engaged in creative practice. All of this can happen in an artist's studio, sometimes simultaneously.

Though they are quite different, technologically and psychedelically or creatively induced altered states of consciousness share something fundamental about presence. Presence happens when you are no longer aware of the mediation between you and the world: it is the intuition of a non-mediated experience.

It already happens every time you speak on the phone, or type a message: the technological device adopts a form of subjectivity, a weird presence, through which you can suddenly hear over an extremely long distance, or send signals into the future. It may manifest when you achieve precision in your work, when your awareness grows to include the tool you're working with. You find yourself overlapping with the technology. You are a cyborg.

Technologies are often designed to hide these workings – privileging 'seamless' or 'frictionless' experience – which risks making you dependent on machines for your dose of presence. But a technologically mediated artwork, crafted gracefully and carefully, can do the opposite. Made with presence by its maker, with all their idiosyncrasies, by a human hand operating powerful machinery, and in acknowledgement of all the other bodies and all the frictions involved in the process, it can actively encourage the development of a new sensitivity. That's when, instead of just showing you a tree, a shadow, or a ghost – however spectacular its visual aspect – it can make you feel like you are in touch with one, or even what it might be like to be one. It's the difference between simulating and summoning.

Newly equipped with such animate capabilities, you become as more-than-human as animals and plants. And after that, this capability can return to you in any other way, even without technology.

There is a technological side to everything, as there is a magical one. I like to think of technology and magic as the yin and yang of the modern world-view. Any successful, mixed-reality artwork – and any presence you experience through mixed reality – also has both a technological and a magical side. The technologically mediated side works on the senses through mechanics and materials, is active and transparent, and can – at least in theory – be analysed and understood. Meanwhile, the magically mediated part seems to come from beyond the senses, is seemingly passive, opaque, mysterious and based on your capacity to open your imagination. At the centre of each of these principles lies a kernel of the other.

Are you working for the machine, is the machine working for you, or are you both working as one? Are you fully present with what you're doing? Are you still aligned with your intentions?

Note to *Mixed Realities*

In this chapter, I am paraphrasing Terence McKenna's description of a mystery from *True Hallucinations*. Other mysteries I mention come from physicist Carlo Rovelli's *White Holes*. For scientists, mystery might propel scientific work. For artists, it can result in exploring these phenomena as an inner, felt or lived experience.

The realisation that we ascribe more-than-human subjectivity to technology was inspired by Emanuele Coccia's aforementioned essay 'Don't Call Me Gaia': 'The entire technological universe is defined by a demonological need. Every time we pick up a phone or computer, leave a voice message or write a text, we turn material reality into a demonic presence, into a form of subjectivity that no longer has an immediate and isomorphic connection with an anatomical corporeality.'

The way I describe and use the idea of presence in this chapter is based, once again, on work by Wijnand IJsselstein on extended reality. His work on 'presence in novel bodies' describes experiments past, present and future that help consciously experience another body as your own through AR and AI. As discussed in *Sitting Is as Magical as Tripping*, I find his ideas on presence equally valuable to understand the experience of psychedelics.

The idea of a technological and a magical side being co-present in all artistic endeavours is inspired by Federico Campagna's *Technic and Magic*: 'Technic and Magic are not mutually exclusive; rather, they are antagonistic world-constructing orientations. Each proposes a different metaphysical structure of reality, and therefore, they constitute alternative modes of inhabiting the world.'

How virtual media and psychedelics are related to peace and rest appears in philosopher Vilém Flusser's *What If?*: 'We have accomplished peace with the help of a certain technique called telematics. This technique allowed us to make all places present such that all events around the world appear to us simultaneously. The simultaneity of all events has resulted in all of them becoming meaningless. [...] The meaninglessness and abstractness of all events is exactly what has facilitated this apathy, the kind of vita contemplativa we live in this resting state. [...] Telematics fulfills what was promised from the beginning, for example, the promise of the eternal peace of the Sabbath, from which humanity emerges from the flow of time to contemplate eternity.'

Artist Patricia Domínguez introduces the notion of channelling, which is itself a study trip technique, in her zine *Technologies of Enchantment*. She discusses and leans on 'inner technologies' as much as 'outer technologies'. Dominguez's work connects the intelligence of computers with that of the Earth. The work demonstrates how objects – such as an ornamented ritual vase – can function as a portal as much as, or even more than, extended-reality software and hardware can: 'As the duck-shaped vase keeps spinning on its axis, the enchanting technology of its geometric patterns brings us to another dimension. We forget about deadlines. We escape from cyclical time. Black lines come forward, white lines recede and a new dimension unfolds before our eyes. Time and space open up in the ceramic vase, while its abstract patterns and geometric lines unfold throughout the body.'

In her work, *Matrix Vegetal*, Domínguez leans on her experiences as a pupil of a local, Indigenous shaman working with plant medicine, as well as her familiarity with virtual media. Combining experimental ethnobotany, oneiric fiction, and technologies of connection both organic and inorganic, the work connects the realm of the more-than-human with that of the technological.

Image on p.170: Patricia Domínguez, Matrix vegetal, *2023. Video installation at Galería Patricia Ready, Santiago de Chile. Commissioned by Screen City Biennial. Photo by Felipe Ugalde, courtesy of the artist.*

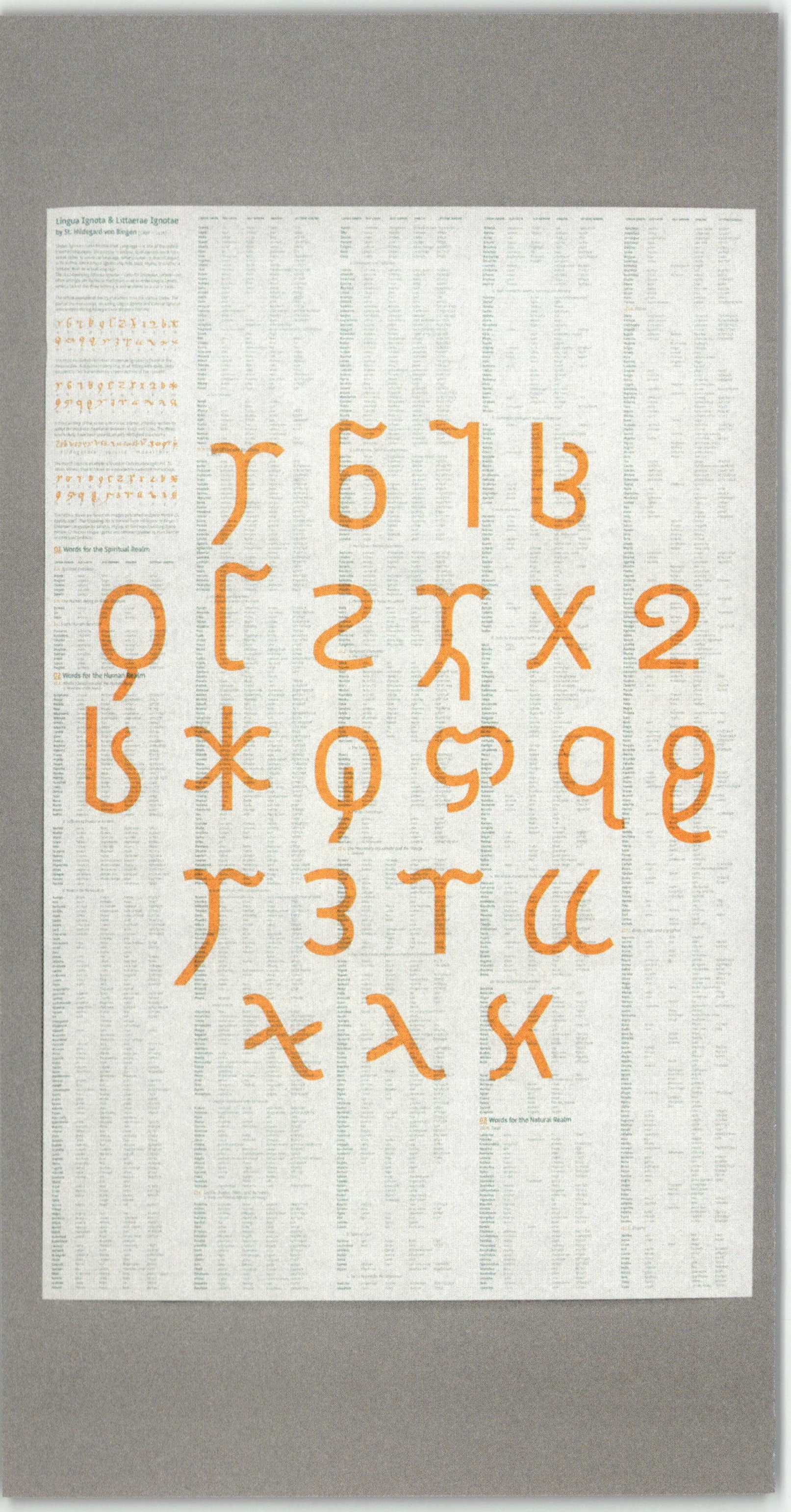
Lingua Ignota & Litterae Ignotae
by St. Hildegard von Bingen
Words for the Spiritual Realm
Words for the Human Realm
Words for the Natural Realm

Knowing What Not to Know

What you can hear and see in a visionary state are not words coming from a human mouth, but glittering flames of meaning. The Earth has a will of her own and she wants your flesh. A wave of particles of light washes over you, and as it is measured, it transubstantiates. You encounter and worship it as solid matter.

Can you hold these visions in all their multiple and contradictory meanings? More difficult still: can you keep your study trip alive in your mind, while you get to know those theories, stories, findings, and judgements by others that appear to contradict yours? Can you hold enough space, with enough humility, for other ways of studying, so that they may co-exist with your own? Can you accept that what might be life-altering revelations to some, might be meaningless to others?

Study trips are performed in pursuit of non-knowledge: in order to create, you often have to give up trying to know, to understand, or to observe objectively, even if only temporarily. Perhaps you choose myth over history, and fantasy over fact, because these are the materials you feel resonate best with your creative work. You may then have a greater talent for forms of non-knowledge. Non-knowledge is a negative capability: the skill to temporarily forget your certainties; to be present subjectively with and in anything that comes to you. If psychedelic study begins with a white light flowing from a vital source, not-knowing is about becoming comfortable in its shadows.

To be sure, suspending for a while objective modes of knowing and critical scrutiny does not mean banning these from your life. Not-knowing can only happen when you acknowledge your limitations and gaps. It comes with the responsibility of educating yourself, learning enough of context, history and verifiable facts, so that your ignorance may become learned, and your not-knowing may remain informed.

If your talent, instead, tends towards objective ways of knowing, you may harbour a desire to accumulate unlimited knowledge. Perhaps you think that everything should, can and will be known, to bring light to places of darkness. But possessing or coveting too much knowledge can produce a similar ignorance as having too little.

A biologist may have a sophisticated understanding of how a tree grows and how its organism functions, but can they also look at a tree while doing away with all that knowledge? For your part, can you witness and be present with a flower, without words, facts, categories of human order? To be vitally alive, in close connection with everything around. This moves beyond the cerebral: it can only be celebrated.

A scientist collecting empirical data and drawing hypotheses from it might have to accept that someone in their future is likely to – and probably will – reveal their theories as incorrect or, at best, incomplete. All major scientific findings from the past have been proven wrong, at least partially, and in any case only relatively right. This is a good indicator of what knowledge actually is, how it escapes us, which is itself a kind of non-knowledge. Not-knowing is an integral part of scientific inquiry.

Knowing with your mind is different from those kinds of knowing that have moved through your entire body, your entire being. You might not think not-knowing is an obvious necessity in your work, and consequently, your capability for meeting it might require some training. It might be even more difficult to let go of the assumption that your preferred form of knowing isn't the only kind there is, without letting go of what you know in its entirety. This too is a negative capability: the capacity to remain open in wonder.

A study trip offers a miraculous opening into a mystery, a moment where any claims to knowledge can be gently set aside. You can let go of your will and stop centring yourself. You can free yourself from striving, measuring and proving. You are learning to rest in not-knowing.

Note to *Knowing What Not to Know*

'Those words that I see and hear in vision are not like words that a human mouth utters, but like a glittering flame,' describes abbess, mystic, composer and philosopher Hildegard of Bingen, and any study tripper will recognise the experience. This chapter is grounded in years of getting acquainted with the subject of not-knowing and is inspired by many references, too many to share here, most of which are collected in the reader *The Library of Not-Knowing.*

Analysis kills, is how Werner Herzog puts it: 'I have a deep aversion to too much introspection, to navel-gazing. [...] If you harshly light every last corner of a house, the house will become uninhabitable,' he writes in his memoir, *Every Man for Himself and God Against All*. While it could be argued that psychedelics temporarily light up the entire house, they do so in ecstasy, not through reason, and the invitation is to keep that light there, in psychedelic space.

In a conversation in *The Dutch Review of Books*, sociologist Philip Gorski and historian and publisher Merlijn Olnon reflect that our current time period, a kind of contemporary Renaissance, may end the same way earlier Renaissances have ended, when enough people choose fantasy over fact, and mythology over history. I would add here that beyond the binary of one or the other, a negative capability needs to be trained, one that combines opposites.

Artist Emma Cocker describes how an artist prepares for the unexpected in a way that could be applied to preparing for a study trip: 'Artistic practice recognises the value of not knowing, less as the preliminary state (of ignorance) preceding knowledge, but as a field of desirable indeterminacy within which to work. Not knowing is an active space within practice, wherein an artist hopes for an encounter with something new or unfamiliar, unrecognisable or unknown. [...] Paradoxically, perhaps, art involves an attempt to smuggle a trace of something infinitely unknowable within the parameters of finite form.' (From 'Tactics for Not Knowing'.)

The Unknown Language, or *Lingua Ignota*, created by Hildegard of Bingen, famously included words and letter forms, yet its purpose is still unknown. To anyone who has studied through psychedelics, the unknown language is a perfect means to approximate that which resists description. Here, the unknowable quality of the language guarantees, up to a point, that there be no claim to knowability over the subjects of study. Anyone who has ever learned a new language knows that the simple fact of learning it, even when it is concerned with entirely worldly things, opens up a new perspective within oneself, shedding new light on everything one previously thought known. Hildegard's new language is neither a formalised exercise, nor is it speaking in tongues. To me, it is an endeavour that brings the rational and the ecstatic into contact. This version of Hildegard's letters is reimagined by type designer Edgar Walthert, while it maintains the original form of the letters.

Image on p.176: Edgar Walthert, Partial Map Hildegard von Bingen – Lingua Ignota, *2022. Foldable map, 210 x 120 x 3 mm. Published by the Palace of Typographic Masonry, courtesy of the artist.*

Combining Different Modes of Knowing

An artist who uses the tools of an astronomer to track and document unknown objects in the sky, and publishes the results as photographs to be meditated upon by their viewers, shares an experiential, subjective form of knowing, without laying claim to verifiable, scientific, external knowledge. A geologist who, on the one hand, develops statistical data on strata of sedimentation, and yet also experiences wonder in the face of such phenomena, may have diagrams end up in a scientific journal, and read poetry on a stage. The double helix structure of the human genome floats into perfect view before the scientist's eyes. Lab experiences, or field work findings, can often exceed, undermine, or challenge the limits of the scientific experiment – just as there are studio encounters, artistic discoveries, and cracks in the fabrics of one's creative activity that exceed the artistic endeavour.

Knowledge is relational; it depends as much on its object, as it does on its subject, the knower. All too often, humans take the primacy of their own subjective experience for granted. It is easy to confuse your knowledge and imagination of the world with the world in and of itself. Whatever the shape of your way of knowing, it is only ever a part of the whole. Looking at the stars above you, what you witness also takes place within you. In your imagination, you see what you are ready and willing to see. Artists work as much with these internal projections as they do with the ones they manipulate externally.

When some obscure, ineffable inner experience presents itself, immeasurable and unverifiable, for a moment it may be grasped as faith. Afterwards, recounting psychedelic experiences to someone else is a way of testing the limits of internal modes of knowing. You may have to reject what you thought was certain, in order to hold space for it as a question.

Internal and external modes of knowing are very different, but they don't exclude each other. They coexist in both time and space. Poetry and science may reach towards the same intuitions via different routes. Just as you cannot make do without reason and criticality, you cannot do without wonder and awe. Knowing something intellectually goes side-by-side with intuition and openness. There is a balance between these approaches, a rhythm; the one offsets the other. A step is both a fall and a landing: learning is constant movement. This involves the body as much as the mind, the brain as much as the gut.

Different forms of knowing may be situated differently, and involve different movements. To learn when to move, and how, is the subject of continuous discipline. You practice it when embarking on a study trip, and you practice it, too, when you dive into critical literature and discussions on subjects you know close to nothing about.

Knowledge, ignorance, and non-knowledge can exist in parallel, and they can transform into each other: by listening, by creating space, and by forgetting. Confronted with your own ignorance, you may learn what you didn't know. If you know so much that it obstructs your creative abilities, you may temporarily forget what you know.

Generally, verifiable, data-based knowledge has been accumulating over the course of human history. But this cannot be said of every time period. Currently, suspicion of externally verified 'scientific' knowledge is growing. Simultaneously, while the value of and practice with more subjective forms of knowing have historically declined, there is renewed interest in these today. This, again, is a question of balance, of not committing only to the one without the other. Learning to correlate internal and external forms of study, you have the opportunity, and perhaps even the responsibility, to create and facilitate spaces for not-knowing, within yourself and in your relations, for yourself and others.

Note to *Combining Different Modes of Knowing*

The biologist and poet I describe here is Patricia Saragüeta, with whom I had an informal conversation about this subject. This coexistence of two forms of knowing opposite to each other is also brilliantly described by novelist John Fowles: 'One might almost call art that branch of science which present science is prevented, by its own constricting tenets and philosophies [...] from reaching.'

Artist Emma Cocker writes about not-knowing as something one has to get acquainted with, building up one's tolerance for it. Combining different forms of knowing, one learns the way one learns to walk: by putting together individual motor skills into a kind of dance.

In Marlen Haushofer's novel *The Wall*, her protagonist writes in her diary (I paraphrase): I knew it already, but only in my head. And so I didn't really believe in it. Truly knowing only happens when knowledge of a particular thing slowly spreads throughout your entire body.

Philosopher Boethius wrote in the sixth century that things are known not according to their natures but according to the nature of the one who is comprehending them. Meghan O'Gieblyn, again, lucidly combines Boethius's insights with those of more contemporary authors.

Physicist Carlo Rovelli: 'We have access only to perspectives. Reality is perhaps nothing other than perspectives. There is no absolute. We are limited, impermanent. And precisely for this reason, to live, to be, as we do, is so light and sweet...'

In his work, artist Trevor Paglen allows different perspectives to align. The objects Paglen photographs are real-life, legitimate UFOs, yet they don't hold the mythic aura of those objects we usually refer to as UFOs. I quote the artist: 'There are about 350 objects in orbit around the Earth that nobody knows what they are. [...] We don't know whether these are naturally occurring or manufactured... They require a lot of concentration to think about, to say anything about. They don't easily lend themselves to fantasy. They tell no stories. I find it both meditative and intensely frustrating to track and photograph these objects. [...] I find their anti-mimetic [sic] qualities reassuring, a respite from a media landscape where everything is trying to capture and weaponize your attention.'

On the more traditional flying saucer-like UFO photographs, he writes: 'I've spent an embarrassingly large amount of time looking at UFO photographs, trying to uncover whether they're "real," "fake," or what, if anything, they depict... In my estimation, their point is that they show each of us what we expect to see or want to see. Creating that tension, showing that contradiction, is what they do. They are image-objects that call forth the projections of whomever views them.'

Image on p.182: Trevor Paglen, UNKNOWN #85217 (Unclassified object near the Cone Nebula), *2023. Silver gelatin LE print, 203.2 x 137.16 cm. © Trevor Paglen, courtesy of the artist and Jessica Silverman Gallery, San Francisco and Pace Gallery, New York.*

Quantum Weirdness and the Limits of Knowledge

Science can be trippy. Two entangled particles on other ends of the Earth, seemingly unconnected, respond to each other. Time runs differently in outer space – or not at all, depending on where you look. Space itself may not be continuous, but built up of the tiniest of quanta, in a woven fabric. Looking out to extraterrestrial events, and focusing down into the smallest possible particles, quantum mechanics and astrophysics have produced deeply weird theories of reality hidden behind the fabric of everyday life – ones it may seem impossible to conceive of.

In classical science, observation happens from a distance, and the observer coolly measures. In quantum physics, any observation affects both the observer and the observed. Any measuring device may hold intelligence, consciousness, and agency in itself. Here, knowing is immediately more-than-human.

Quantum physics shakes the foundations of many epistemologies, as do study trips. In the ecstatic, psychedelic state, all measurement stops. Observing from this state is no different from being observed. Object and subject overlap. In a study trip, you see through the veil that hides psychedelic weirdness from everyday life. What is often described as counterintuitive in quantum physical scientific findings and theories, to a study tripper may make complete, intuitive sense.

You experience what it would be like to move along a minute weft of spatial particles; you jump from one quantum to the next; you float through the nothingness that may lie in between. Time becomes an eternal, perfect presence, or you find yourself in even weirder places, not even speculated about by theorists. What would a star dream of?

Any rational understanding is completely out of the question. Visiting hyperspace doesn't give you new knowledge of the kind that builds rockets. But non-knowledge can inspire the quest for actual, positive, real-world knowledge too. It can propel you to explore, to search for answers while contemplating deeper mysteries.

When you manage to relate the two, the exercise brings you knowledge about knowledge itself: it can show you what knowledge cannot know, without the need to discard it. If psychedelic study has one single, verifiable benefit for everyone, it is the capacity to point out the limits of knowledge.

You feel the sun shining through the canopy of a primeval forest long before there were humans; you see the twilight burst into colours through the stained-glass windows of an alien church. The presences around you bathe in light. If these beings are representations of things happening in your own life, then representations are as alive as you and me. The human body is made of countless other entities, each within their own ecologies and with their own entanglements. Through all of them, within the confines of your own body, you may encounter the universe.

I don't know if I experience the same things on psychedelics or in meditation as you do; I don't know if it is possible to truly know someone else, to truly know myself, and I certainly don't know what the mysterious space of psychedelics truly is. Before I come back from a study trip, a deity gives me a drink that makes me forget: when I'm back, I realise there are no fixed answers, only incrementally better formulated questions.

By knowing nothing, I can reach the limits of my mind. What comes up in psychedelic study presents itself as an opening. What remains is what I am able to make of it. And it seems that the more fantastic and surreal the images, the more vital for everyday life they become.

Note to *Quantum Weirdness and the Limits of Knowledge*

Here again Meghan O'Gieblyn: 'The ability to simultaneously observe an electron's position and momentum would require the impossible: perfect presence in a single moment in time. The very nature of observation requires the observer to generalise.'

The myth of the Western, reductionist, scientific mind has famously little place for the sacred. When it does, it places it within history or attributes it to cultures it simultaneously others. Yet many have successfully combined this mythical Western worldview with another, equally mythical worldview that is at times religious or spiritual. A very good example may be found in the essays of rocket scientist Freeman Dyson. While Dyson studied and worked in physics, he is clear to communicate the limits of scientific knowledge. In *Dreams of Earth and Sky*, he writes: 'The public has a distorted view of science because children are taught in school that science is a collection of firmly established truths. In fact, science is not a collection of truths. It is a continuing exploration of mysteries. Wherever we go exploring in the world around us, we find mysteries.'

It takes someone who knows a lot, to acknowledge that there is much they don't know. As a writer, I am hopelessly uninformed on Dyson's scientific work and understanding, yet I have at least some form of understanding of all that I don't know about it. This informed not-knowing allows me to see my own forms of knowing, expressed through poetry and art, as closely aligned with Dyson's description of science's mysteries.

After the wildest explorations during study trips, 'you get Meng Po's soup of forgetting' (a saying from Taoist folklore), and you can begin the process of aligning your experiences with other forms of knowing.

In this chapter, what I know of measurement in quantum physics has been partly based on a reading of *Meeting the*

Universe Halfway, by physicist and philosopher of science Karen Barad. Barad suggests that knowing is not a capacity that is 'the exclusive birthright of the human. Knowing is a material practice, a specific engagement of the world where part of the world becomes differentially intelligible to another part of the world in its differential accountability to or for that of which it is a part.' Barad describes how the idea that sentience, consciousness, and intelligence are all necessary components of a measuring device, emerges from the strangeness of quantum physics.

One of the largest church windows in Europe is found in Alkmaar, in the Netherlands. Artist Fiona Tan designed its new stained-glass windows, basing the design on how the sunlight enters the church and reflects the particular colours, movements, and the landscape. Another influence for the artist was the kaleidoscope, a tool she remembers from her childhood, when, after World War II, she was given a few fragments of coloured glass from the Reims Cathedral by her uncle. The colourful patterns of the window are made from antique coloured glass, and were composed using algorithms. The proto-filmic play of light inside the church is an experience closely related to what one traditionally comes to church for. It reminds me of how rays of light might be glimpsed in particular patches of primeval forests. The work can reconnect a viewer to the surrounding landscape, the local sunlight, other visitors, and even computer algorithms, temporarily showing the limits of fixed perspectives and reductionist forms of knowing, without having to discard anything, or to impose any dogma.

Image on p.188: Fiona Tan, The Great Window, *2023, Saint Laurence Church, Alkmaar. Photo: E. Boschman, courtesy of the artist.*

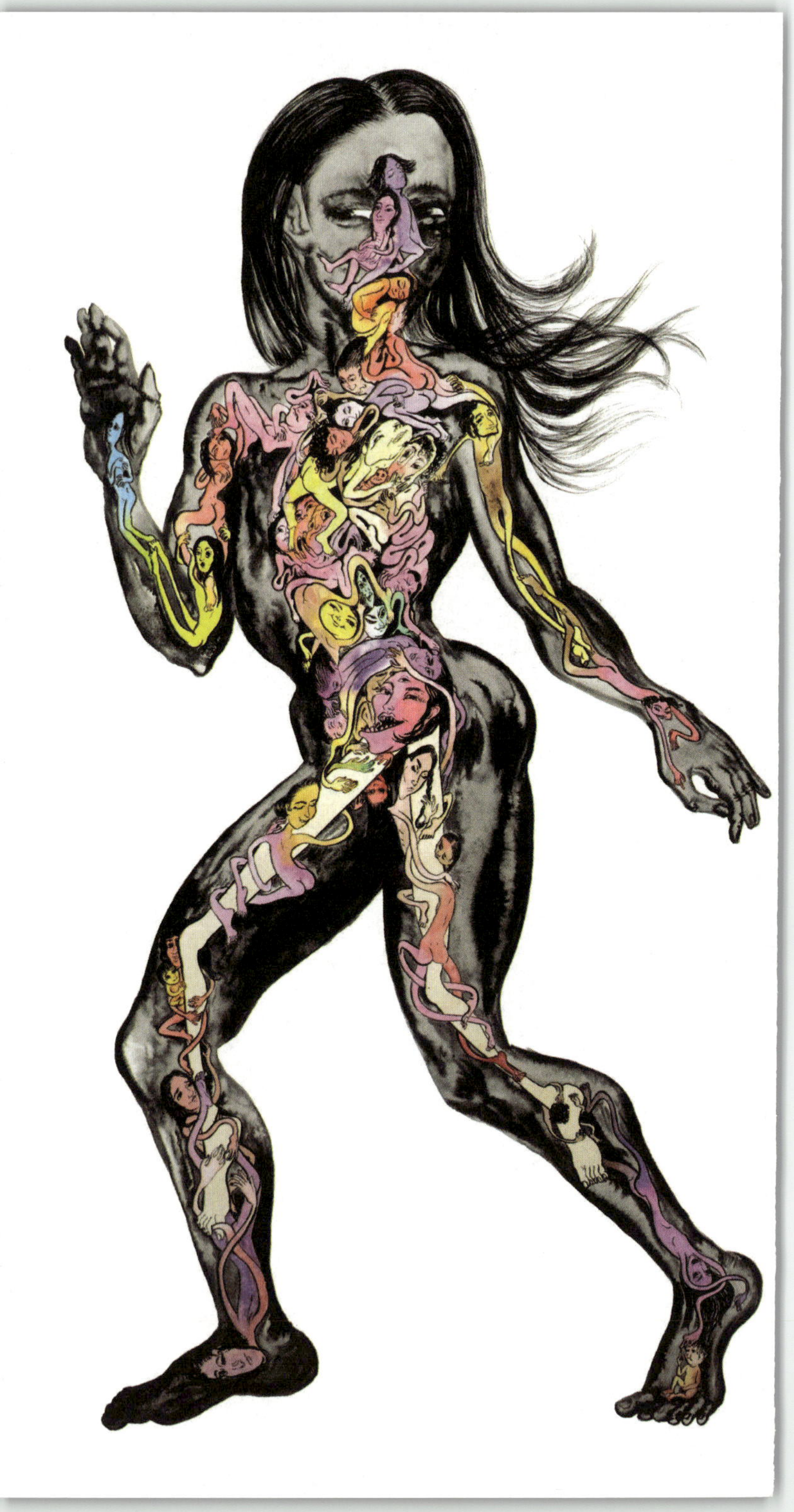

Afterword

When you practice not-knowing, you train faith. Often, when people talk of faith, what they mean is blind faith, or dogmatism. But all faith really is, is a deep trust, not founded on authority, experience or knowledge. Faith is not the same as knowing: it's not-knowing. It's accepting that we cannot imagine what reality might be, yet trusting in what these realities can and will germinate. There really is no end to what may flourish through a study trip.

Psychedelics are sometimes known as 'becoming ghost' or 'death by astonishment', evoking a metaphorical death. Strong psychedelics are often compared to near-death experiences. What can you learn by 'practicing dying'?

Psychedelics are successfully involved in learning to let go where letting go is absolutely necessary:

in hospicing, mourning or trauma treatment. In the literature on shamanism, the experience of a metaphorical death – whether through accident, trance, substances or techniques – is described as having an initiatory function. During a study trip, the ego dies, the personal self that discerns between us and them, and you and me, is temporarily no more. Yet if this is death, you are at the same time, uniquely and incredibly alive. Life and death and love are all one. Ancestors meet progeny. There are no thoughts, only a big, still light. The past and the future are here, more present and more real than the actual moment of experience.

Coming back from the land of the dead after a study trip does something to any subconscious fear of death or death drive you may have. Study trips can teach you how to live in eternity – not by denying, repressing or being afraid of death, nor by longing for any form of afterlife. Denial can mask a hidden death wish, while a secret longing for death can easily be a symptom of alienation from the living landscapes of this life. A metaphorical death, experienced in a study trip, can help us surrender to death's certainty, as much as to its mystery.

Our world is full of violence, death and fanaticism. Simultaneously, death is feared, foreclosed and hidden away from discourse and consciousness. In all their weirdness, study trips – and the works of art that may result from them – are exercises in surrender to both not knowing and not being. A new space grows between two extreme positions towards death. Where there is inner turbulence, it encourages new openness to the everyday world. Where there is alienated projection, it facilitates inner expansion.

Today it is too easy to experience individual ecstasy: most of us spend a disproportionate amount of time virtually possessed by our technological apparatuses. What we can re-learn through a study trip is how a different kind of ecstasy can become consciously devoted, dedicated and experienced in relationship with those real-world subjectivities, human and more-than-human, surrounding us. In a sense, 'individual ecstasy' is a contradiction in terms: even the most isolated and alienated social-media user is still always connected to the intentions of tech companies, to the people designing their experiences and devices, and even to the landscapes from which technology's raw materials and rare earths are extracted. The connections are as innumerable as they are hidden from view.

But letting go never ends, and neither does finding yourself reborn. Revelatory as they are, ecstasies are not an end in and of themselves. The journey becomes about how you are able to translate them into real-world actions.

Seeds die, too, in order for new forms to grow. Practicing dying is learning to liberate constrained energy, to exist within the continuously changing relationships of all that surrounds us. Every step we take can be used to forge more or less reciprocal connections. This is a quest that seeks the garden, that garden of earthly delights, where all relationships are given space and acknowledgement, that garden that every so often shows up in art, and where we may sometimes, all of a sudden and wherever we are, already find ourselves.

Note to *Afterword*

'Death by astonishment' is a famous description of psychedelic ego-death by Terence McKenna. 'Becoming ghost' is, instead, how Yanomami shaman Davi Kopenawa describes it.

In Marlen Haushofer's *The Wall*, the protagonist describes what she sees when exhausted and near death: 'I had no thoughts, no memories, there was only the big, silent, snowy light. I knew this feeling could be dangerous for a lonely person, but I couldn't muster any strength to resist it. [S]ometimes the desire to go into the white and painless silence is very great.'

I'm citing Werner Herzog too, from his talk and article 'On the Absolute, the Sublime, and Ecstatic Truth'. He writes: 'What constitutes reality became a greater mystery to me than it had been. [...] In the fine arts, in music, literature, and cinema, it is possible to reach a deeper stratum of truth – a poetic, ecstatic truth, which is mysterious and can only be grasped with effort; one attains it through vision, style, and craft. [...] We can't disregard the factual; it has normative power. But it can never give us the kind of illumination, the ecstatic flash, from which Truth emerges.'

Many have written about learning how to sit still, among whom mathematician Blaise Pascal, who, in his *Pensées*, lamented: 'All of humanity's problems stem from man's inability to sit quietly in a room alone.'

On faith, reality and fiction, I quote Vilém Flusser (*On Fiction*): 'What if reality resides neither in the object nor the subject, but perhaps is found in the relationship between the two? [...] Our epoch pretends to be mad. Yet, deep down, it knows what reality is. The kind of reality that neither experience nor knowledge can provide, since both are misleading. The kind of reality that only faith can provide.'

From Simone Weil's *Decreation*, I borrowed ideas on how the seed has to die in order to liberate the energy it bears within it, so that with this energy, new forms may be developed.

Saelia Aparicio comments on her drawing *Ethereal Entraña* – ethereal entrail, or inner being: 'Inside I'm a ghost made of dust; it wants to fly but tends to settle in dark corners.'

Image on p.194: Saelia Aparicio, Ethereal Entraña, *2026. Ink and watercolour on paper, 64 x 56 cm. Courtesy of the artist.*

Extras

NARCOTOURISM / KBH 5-II MAY 1996

I will walk in the city* over the course of seven days, under the influence of a different drug** each day. My trip will be recorded through ~~photographs~~, notes, and any other media that become relevant.

*the *project* is about being physically present in a place, while mentally elsewhere.

**dosage: drugs were consumed in order to maintain a continuous effect for 14 h.a day.

May 5 ....Spirits (I)
May 6 ....Hashish (2)
May 7 ....Speed (3)
May 8 ....Heroin (4)
May 9 ....Cocaine (5)
May 10 ....Valium (6)
May II ....Ecstasy (7)
(8)

(I) Spirits. (due to practical problems in finding the stuff, I decide to start with local liquors and alcohol). Difficulties in connecting mentally with my physical state. Inner resistance. Inability to trust my reflexes or sight. I walk clumsily among many strange occurences.

(2) Hashish. Slow motion. Awareness of every muscle in action. Everything is enormously funny. Soundless speech. Walking with my eyes closed. A pastrami sandwich tastes heavenly.

(3) Speed. Deambulatory paranoia. Cold feet. I fear the signs of my own presence, and avoid encounters on the street. As I walk, I always keep a familiar spot in sight.

(4) Heroin. Feeling of inner warmth which helps me break the ice and feel attuned to the place. A sequence of frozen images as I walk along the Danube. The effects fade fast, but they return at the end of the day. Difficulty breathing at night.

(5) Cocaine. Awareness of a change of state, but not followed by a visual echo. Auditory acuity enhanced. Appetite gone Smoking diminished. At night, nausea and thirst.

(6) Valium. Weariness. Aesthenia. Indifference to context. Regular smoking. Frequent pissing and occasional vomiting. While walking, bittersweet memories pop up at regular intervals.

(7) Ecstasy. Visual brightening and erotic impulses. My shoes move and I feel the urge to walk out. Everything I turn to moves, not physically but conceptually. I feel like the epicenter of the world.

(8) The journey was followed by a period of depression. I understood it but could not help sinking into it.

Study Trip Diary

The following template with questions is intended to be used regularly. Keep track of your answers to these questions, and compare those to your answers from a previous entry. Similarly, adjust the passages that look ahead to the next session.

Sessions

(1) What techniques and/or substances will you be using?
(2) How often?
(3) What kind of duration/dosage are you aiming for?

Experiments

(1) Which new practical elements will you want to implement?
(2) What new things will you be trying in your creative work, that align with your study trip sessions?

Intentions

(1) Are there any specific subjectivities you would like to study?
(2) Are there any particular presences you would like to dedicate a session to?

Community

(1) With whom and where will you be organising your session?
(2) Will you be hosting and/or joining?
(3) Where do you source your techniques; what or who are you following?
(4) Where do you grow or find your substances; who are you sustaining?

Ceremony

(1) Are you following a format of ceremony developed by others, or are you coming up with your own rituals?
(2) What can you contribute to existing rituals?
(3) Which art forms might be involved?

Trip Report

(1) Will you be conversing, drawing or writing afterwards?
(2) What do any reports from previous experiences tell you now?

Diary

(1) What predictions, simulations or thought processes stood out to you?
(2) What perspectives have you been missing until now?
(3) What assumptions have you been able to record?
(4) What perspectives can you glean from your changing assumptions?

Index

Notes Pages

NOTES PAGES

NOTES PAGES

NOTES PAGES

NOTES PAGES

NOTES PAGES

Colophon

Set Margins' #97
Study Trip: Psychedelics for Research and Art
ISBN: 978-90-836052-9-6
Written and designed by Dirk Vis
Edited by Lucia Pietroiusti
Proofread by Johanna Monk
Printed by PBtisk
Typeface: MD Lórien by Mass-Driver
Cover image: Job Wouters, *Study Trip*, 2025. Ink on paper, 20 x 11.5 cm. Courtesy of the artist.
Image on p.202: Francis Alÿs, *Narcotourism (diary)*, 1996. Typewriter ink and graphite on paper, 32 x 46 cm. Courtesy of the artist.

NIAS | Netherlands Institute for Advanced Study in the Humanities and Social Sciences

This work was supported by The Netherlands Institute for Advanced Study in the Humanities and Social Sciences (NIAS).

The thoughts on ornamentation from the chapter *Through the Portal* come from the text *The Redemptive Qualities of Ornament* published by *The Palace of Typographic Masonry* in 2022.

www.dirkvis.work
Set Margins'
www.setmargins.press